The Durrells of Corfu

MICHAEL HAAG

The *Durrells* of Corfu

MICHAEL HAAG

P

PROFILE BOOKS

First published in Great Britain
in 2017 by Profile Books:
3 Holford Yard, Bevin Way
London WC1X 9HD
www.profilebooks.com

1 3 5 7 9 10 8 6 4 2

Typeset in Sabon 10.5/14
to a design by Henry Iles.

A CIP catalogue record for this book is available from the British Library.
224pp

ISBN 978-1781257883
e-ISBN 978-1782833307

Printed and bound by CPI Group (UK) Ltd, Croydon, CR0 4YY
on Forest Stewardship Council (mixed sources) certified paper.

MIX
Paper from
responsible sources
FSC® C020471

To Kenneth and Maureen Maguire

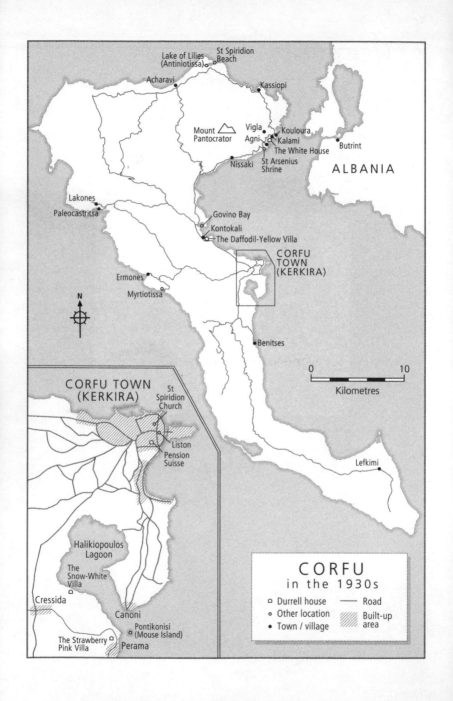

St Spiridion
Beach
Lake of Lilies
(Antiniotissa)
Acharavi
Kassiopi
Mount
Pantocrator
Vigla
Agni
Kouloura
Kalami
The White House
Nissaki
St Arsenius
Shrine
ALBANIA
Butrint
Lakones
Paleocastritsa
Govino Bay
Kontokali
The Daffodil-Yellow Villa
CORFU
TOWN
(KERKIRA)
Ermones
Myrtiotissa
N
Benitses
0   10
Kilometres
Lefkimi

CORFU TOWN
(KERKIRA)
St
Spiridion
Church
Liston
Pension
Suisse

Halikiopoulos
Lagoon
The
Snow-White
Villa
Cressida
Canoni
Pontikonisi
(Mouse Island)
The Strawberry
Pink Villa
Perama

CORFU
in the 1930s
▢ Durrell house   —— Road
○ Other location   ▨ Built-up
● Town / village   area

Contents

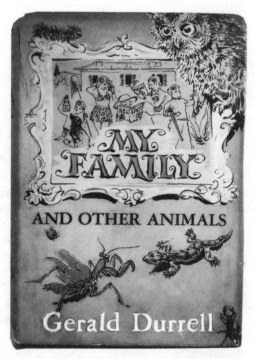

The first edition of *My Family and Other Animals*.

Introduction: **The Durrells of Corfu**

IN 1935 LOUISA DURRELL AND HER FOUR CHILDREN – Lawrence (Larry), Leslie, Margaret (Margo) and Gerald (Gerry) – went to live in Corfu. The years that followed were made famous in Gerald Durrell's much-loved *My Family and Other Animals* and in *Birds, Beasts and Relatives* and *The Garden of the Gods*, the other volumes of his *Corfu Trilogy*. Gerry's older brother Lawrence, who achieved world renown with *The Alexandria Quartet*, also wrote his own beautifully observed book about Corfu, *Prospero's Cell*.

'We had arrived at a place that was to be of enormous influence over all of us,' Gerry wrote of the family's reaction to Corfu. 'It was like being allowed back into Paradise.'

In *My Family and Other Animals* Gerry gives the impression that the family came to Corfu almost on a whim, selling up their house and sailing into the unknown to escape rainy summer days in England and stuffed-up noses. But what he does not mention, and neither does Larry in *Prospero's Cell*, was the tragedy. They laughed and wrote beautifully of their island idyll, but nobody mentioned what had really brought them to the island – the sudden death of their father in India, the devastating effect it had on their mother, and the yearning to restore something lost.

But the brightness and colour and the freedom they discovered in Corfu lifted their spirits. The island possessed the softness of an Italian landscape, the warmth and fragrance of the Mediterranean, the idiosyncrasy of Greece – an intensity of sensations they had not known since leaving India. For the Durrells, after their years in England struggling with their family tragedy, it was a rebirth. Protective of their family unity, the children never pushed their disorder too far, allowing their mother to preside over a happy anarchy. For each of the Durrells, Corfu was a healing.

This book takes a fresh look at the story of the Durrells in Corfu. Individual members of the Durrell family, and the Durrell Wildlife Conservation Trust in Jersey, have provided the author with letters and reminiscences of their lives in India, England and Corfu, as well as later, and also many family photographs. These allow the family to speak for themselves, presenting a new and revealing narrative, and provide a detailed account of the family before Corfu, and during their stay on the island, and in the immediate aftermath of war. And not only the family but figures who played a crucial part in their lives, like Larry's friend and Gerry's mentor Theodore Stephanides; the outsized character of Spiro Americanos, taxi-driver and all-round fixer; and the American writer Henry Miller, who visited Larry in Corfu towards the end of the Durrells' stay and began his own journey there, his discovery of Greece, which he recorded in the best book he ever wrote, *The Colossus of Maroussi*.

The Durrells of Corfu concludes with an epilogue which traces what happened to almost everyone who had been part of the story in Corfu and provides a summary of the remarkable careers of Larry and Gerry, including the realisation of Gerry's childhood dream, the founding of the Durrell Zoo in Jersey.

While the book is not a guide to the Durrells' island, it can serve to allow the reader to follow in the footsteps of the family, discovering the villas and places they knew and wrote about.

Larry himself described how he and Gerry returned years later to Corfu and retraced their own footsteps by joining a tour.

> I don't know how posthumous you can feel, but my brother and I put on dark glasses and funny hats and we went on one of these trips, and I've never heard so much misinformation about our family and in such strange French. I think they were all Syrians. Anyway, we drank Coca-Cola in our own honour and sneaked off back to town.

The Durrells themselves were masters of fabulation. All of the children were great storytellers and embroiderers of tales. They complained about Gerry's *My Family and Other Animals* – Margo in particular – even as they happily appropriated each other's stories and, where necessary, invented new ones. According to a close friend of Gerry's, *Birds Beasts and Relatives*, the second volume of *The Corfu Trilogy*, was filled with leftover anecdotes so improbable that Gerry thought no one would believe them, while his third volume, *The Garden of the Gods*, was packed with stories which even if true, Gerald himself could not believe. As for the first volume, *My Family and Other Animals*, and also Larry's *Prospero's Cell*, Margo summed it up when she said, 'I never know what's fact and what's fiction in my family'.

This book ventures into those magical days in Corfu before the war, and in trying to address Margo's problem sheds new light on old stories and uncovers fresh stories that are often just as strange and fascinating and funny.

* * *

Top: the wedding of Lawrence Samuel Durrell and Louisa Dixie in Roorkee, 1910. Bottom: the Durrell family with visiting relatives in Jamshedpur, c.1920: Lawrence Samuel (far left), Louisa (far right), Larry (in shorts, standing), Margo and Leslie (sitting on the steps); Gerry was not yet born.

Chapter 1: **India**

THE DURRELLS WERE COLONIALS, all of them born in India. England was their cultural homeland, but Louisa in particular thought of India as her real home. Louisa – 'Mother' in *My Family and Other Animals* – was born Louisa Dixie in Roorkee in the Punjab, in 1887, and was raised in a large extended family there, all long settled in India. Her parents had been born in the Punjab, and she would marry Lawrence Samuel Durrell, also Indian-born, a brilliant and ambitious civil engineer, and travel with him across the Raj. All the Durrell children were born in India, too, and the colours, scents and sounds of the subcontinent would shape their sensibilities.

In India, however, Louisa suffered two tragedies. First, the loss of Margery, her second child, from diphtheria. Then in 1928 the catastophe of her husband's sudden death from a brain haemorrhage. Advised by friends in the British community that India was no place to raise a young family, Louisa set sail within weeks of her husband's death for 'home', bereaved and lost, with a fatherless family to raise.

* * *

Lawrence Samuel Durrell's father was a country boy, born out of wedlock, who had left Suffolk when he was eighteen and rose to the rank of major in the British Indian Army. Louisa Dixie's family had been in India a generation longer. Her grandfather came to teach at Thomason College of Civil Engineering in Roorkee – the first college of engineering in the British Empire (and now the prestigious Indian Institute of Technology). Her father was head clerk and accountant for the workshop and foundry that maintained the Ganges Canal, a vast British-built irrigation project that transformed the Punjab into the breadbasket of India.

Lawrence Samuel was eighteen when he first met Louisa at the Dixies' home in Roorkee; he knew her older brother John Dixie from studying at Thomason College and would join the Dixie family in tennis, dancing and amateur theatricals. There he found himself attracted to John's sister, a dreamy girl, barely sixteen, with a mischievous sense of fun, who stood at least a head shorter than her tall and earnest visitor.

After leaving Thomason College in 1904, Lawrence Samuel went to work for the North Western Railway as an assistant engineer, supervising the construction of a bridge across the Sutlej, the greatest of the Punjab's five rivers, a difficult but successful task which, in 1909, when he was just twenty-five,

Thomason College of Civil Engineering, Roorkee, India.

won him promotion to district engineer at Karnal in the Punjab, where he had responsibility for almost every construction project in the area. In 1910, with growing confidence in his career, he married Louisa and took her to Jullundur, astride the main railway line towards the Khyber Pass and Afghanistan, where he had been appointed the Railway's district engineer. It was there, a year later, that their first child, Lawrence George Durrell – Larry – was born.

For the next two decades, Lawrence Samuel and Louisa and their growing family would migrate from one railway project to the next across the breadth of the Raj, which in those days included all of present-day India as well as Pakistan, Bangladesh and Burma – from Jullundur in the Punjab to the jungles of Arakan Burma on the far side of the Bay of Bengal; from Mymensingh on the flood plain of the Brahmaputra River up to Kurseong in the forested hill country below Darjeeling perched among the snow peaks of the Himalayas.

* * *

Larry's earliest memories were of the monsoon rains at Buthi-daung, at the head of the Mayu River, deep in the interior of Arakan, a region in western Burma, a thousand miles east of his birthplace at Jullundur. He was nine months old when he travelled there with his parents – by rail across the breadth of India and then by steamer across the Bay of Bengal. At the Burmese coast they boarded a side-paddler which meandered upriver through a shifting alluvial landscape of paddy fields and forests and swamps and flimsy reed huts where everything seemed hidden and remote. As the sun went down they landed at Buthidaung, a village of three or four thousand people, its main street a dirt path leading off into the paddy fields, its houses of wood and reed clinging to the riverbank.

Here Larry would remain until he was three, living with his mother and a Buddhist *ayah* or nanny, while his father,

Larry with his ayah in Burma.

still only twenty-eight years old, mastered a labour force of Pathans, a rugged people from the warlike tribes of the North-West Frontier Province of British India, to build a railway through the mountains. Assailed by leeches, flies and mosquitoes, they cleared their way through jungle inhabited by deer, tigers and wild boar, carved miles of gradients out of the mountain flanks and cut two railway tunnels through the rock, connecting the interior directly with the coast as part of the

British project which was developing Arakan into one of the major rice exporting regions in the world.

Lawrence Samuel was away for weeks at a time, leaving Louisa and Larry on their own. In the evening the village was shrouded by a dense mist rising from the river; in the morning it would clear and the day became as bright and shimmering as a watercolour, but that was outside the rainy season. For five months of the year, from June to October, it rained so continuously and hard that it seemed the whole world would be washed away. 'The ground was rapidly becoming a living clot of humidity, and the ravines mere waterways for the passage of such debris as the wind had torn from the hillsides,' Larry recalled of the onset of the monsoon. 'At the approach of that season the forests began to huddle together and grip the disintegrating earth more firmly with their roots.' Louisa knew the monsoon in the Punjab but here the rainfall was fifty times greater and there were no canals to control the floods, yet according to Larry his mother was happy here, and he himself was a confident and robust boy, able to withstand the perils of disease and extremes of climate in Arakan Burma.

* * *

Towards the end of 1915, Lawrence Samuel took up a new engineering post, this time in East Bengal (now Bangladesh), and settled Louisa, eight months pregnant, and Larry, who was nearly four years old, into their new home. This was in Mymensingh, at that time a backwater town of twenty thousand Muslims and Hindus situated on the west bank of a silted-up and barely navigable channel of the Brahmaputra.

The district was a vast alluvium planted with fields of jute and rice which was dependent on poor roads trafficked by pack animals or on the old channel of the Brahmaputra River, which was navigable only during the rainy season, when daytime temperatures were torrid and the atmosphere was sodden. Motor cars and electricity were unknown. Lawrence Samuel's task was to carry a railway line across the Brahmaputra that would connect the district to Calcutta and other major ports and markets, contributing immensely to the development of the region.

In November, just after the monsoon had passed, Louisa gave birth to a baby girl, Margery. The following March, a month after Larry turned four, and as temperatures were rising and the rains were starting again, the baby became ill with a mild sore throat; within days she was overwhelmed by fever, her neck swelling until she could no longer swallow and could barely breathe. She was gripped by the full force of diphtheria. In those times before the discovery of antibiotics, the Medical Officer could do nothing and, two days later, cradled by her mother, watched by Larry, the child suffocated to death.

The shock of the death had a lasting effect on Louisa and also on Larry, who despite his naturally ebullient nature would always feel the vulnerability of his own existence and the ease by which the world around him could be undermined. 'Why do people die?' he would write in a little-known early autobiographical novel of a boy growing up in India called *Pied Piper of Lovers*, a novel he wrote in England just before going to Corfu. The boy in the novel is a strong, healthy child, yet he is aware that people not unlike himself become ill and die and their parents can do nothing.

* * *

Lawrence Samuel's work continued to take him away from his afflicted family for long stretches of time and Louisa took to the habit of drinking too much gin and began to seek comfort in the world of lost spirits. And when the following year Louisa gave birth to a second son, Leslie, in the midst of a cholera epidemic, she was terrified of losing him. She would always be over-protective towards Leslie and always willing to indulge him.

Relief for the young family, however, came when Lawrence Samuel accepted the position of executive engineer of the Darjeeling Himalayan Railway in the healthier climate of Kurseong, amidst tea plantations in the foothills of the Himalayas where Margaret, the Margo of Gerry's *My Family and Other Animals*, was born in 1919.

Though Leslie and Margaret were too young to remember anything at all of Kurseong, the place was Larry's childhood home from the age of six to nearly nine. The town was a centre of the tea trade and clung to the lower slopes of the Himalayas, where the native growth of forest and scrub was being cut away by tea gardens which wrapped round the hillsides in terraces. Kurseong's elevation at nearly five thousand feet introduced Larry to flora and fauna he had not known when living in the plain. 'The garden was full of all manner of strange flowers that he had not seen before', he recalled in *Pied Piper of Lovers* his early autobiographical novel:

> Half a dozen different varieties of beetle, ranging from the walnut-sized coproghagous one, to the sheeny

The Batasia Loop, built by Lawrence Samuel, reduces the gradient on the approach to Darjeeling in the Himalayas.

grey-green rose-beetles. Caterpillars were enormous, banded with every colour of the rainbow; moths and butterflies, blue, brown, slate-coloured, and bright yellow, busied themselves all day about the corners of the bushes. He explored these mysteries as thoroughly as he was able, wandering all day long through the deserted pathways, upon the carpets of moss, whispering to himself or talking to his companion, the *ayah*.

The pleasure Larry drew from his surroundings and his acute observation of flowers and insects would later be repeated in Corfu by his youngest brother Gerry, who would be encouraged and guided by his older brother. 'As he neared home,' Larry wrote of his alter ego in his novel, 'a huge Colombian moth, furred blue, and measuring about six inches from wingtip to wing-tip, fluttered across his path and away into the evening. He cursed himself bitterly for a fool. He should have brought his butterfly net.'

* * *

A photo taken near the Durrells' home at Kurseong in the Himalayas.

Railway building in the mountains did not hold Lawrence Samuel for long. In 1920 he resigned his position and brought his family down from Kurseong to the hot plains at Jamshedpur, 150 miles west of Calcutta, where the soil, red with iron ore, was feeding the beginning of India's industrial revolution. Here he founded his own civil engineering and construction company, Durrell & Co.

By the time the Durrells arrived at Jamshedpur, the one-time village in the midst of a steaming jungle had already burgeoned into an industrial town of over 50,000 people, with projected development projects set to increase the numbers fourfold within the next few years. The steel factory alone employed over 25,000 people. But conditions were primitive and the terrain still half wild. Local tigers, enraged at the destruction of their forest home, had killed two Indian labourers, and an elephant, driven berserk by the disturbance and the noise, smashed a number of workers' huts to pieces.

Durrell & Co. won a contract to build a tin-plate mill, a brick-making plant, an office building, a 300-bed hospital complete with diagnostic and operating facilities, and over 400 workers' houses, each with its garden, for the Tata family who as philanthropists as well as entrepreneurs were determined to make Jamshedpur a model town, socially and technologically far in advance of any other city in India. The Tata Steel plant had by 1939 become the largest in the British Empire and today the city is one of the most advanced industrial and high-tech cities in India, home to the multinational Tata company, the owners of Jaguar, Land Rover and Tetley Tea.

Gerald – Gerry – was born at Jamshedpur on 7 January 1925. Louisa was thirty-eight and Lawrence Samuel forty. 'His arrival did not disturb us children at all,' remembered Margaret. 'Gerry was just the baby, given over to our Hindu *ayah*, carefully watched by Mother', to guard against the common practice of dipping her fingers in opium to soothe the cries of a restless child. His father seemed a remote figure. 'I would see him twice a day for half an hour and he would tell me stories about the Three Bears. I knew he was my daddy but I was on much greater terms of intimacy with Mother and my *ayah*.'

Larry, the oldest of the Durrell children, was nearly thirteen when Gerry was born and had been shipped off to school in England two years previously. The family had gone with

Margo and Leslie with Larry, on a visit to England, 1923.

him – their first visit to England – to enrol him at St Olave's grammar school in Bermondsey, on the south bank of the Thames in London (he later moved to St Edmund's public school in Canterbury). 'Lawrence', Margo said (she always called him Lawrence), 'was deposited at school in England, feeling abandoned and bearing a grudge against his parents. I felt I never knew my brother Lawrence as a young boy. We returned to India, to home.' Larry never saw India again. He never knew Gerry in India and hardly knew Leslie and Margo there either. 'His presence', remembered Margo, who was four when Larry went to England, 'was only felt by me as a passing blond, boisterous elder brother.'

Larry had, in fact, been away from the family for much of the previous three years, at St Joseph's College, a Jesuit school in Darjeeling, so that when Margo recalled the way things were at home in Jamshedpur Larry was like an absent memory. 'Nursery was our kingdom until the magic hour of teatime at 4pm, when we children would be washed and dressed in clean clothes and presented to Mother and Father in the drawing room. I do not remember Lawrence at all in those times; he must have been away in Darjeeling.'

But, Margo added, 'I think Lawrence experienced the most glamorous and best part of our life as children in India.' Whereas his siblings' memories only went back to Jamshedpur, to the days when the family's circumstances became more settled and prosperous, the surroundings more ordinary, Larry shared the early trials and adventures of his mother and father.

* * *

The Durrells' house in Jamshedpur was a long low bungalow with flowers and greenery climbing up the pillars of the verandah. The family's tailor sat cross-legged in the shade of the verandah whirling his sewing machine, while indoors the air was stirred and cooled by fans and punkah wallahs. The bungalow was set within a large and beautifully kept garden and beyond it was a compound to shelter the servants.

The garden was the setting for birthdays and Christmases, Margo remembering 'magical times with marquees, lots of guests, children, music, presents, rollicking party games, wonderful party dresses and the cooks producing their best from the kitchen'. A snake charmer would appear with cobras rising from round baskets, 'swaying to the sweet call of the crude bamboo pipes, surrounded by happy laughing children'. And once they were joined by an Indian banging a drum followed by a large brown bear on which the children were allowed to ride around the garden.

When Margo spoke of the joys and escapades of her childhood she meant Leslie and herself, so close to one another in age. 'We were conspirators most times when not enemies and beating each other up. We were always doing things like trying to poison the governess, an English Catholic, a tough spinster and an ogre in the eyes of Leslie and me. She was a pious lady who spent her free moments supplicating the Lord in prayer. We were put directly under her responsibility much to our alarm and war was declared at once. We were given lessons by the governess and we hated it.' After wishing for her death they would creep into her room in the mornings to see if she was still breathing. Or they would plot to creep off 'to forbidden territories, to the canal, a slow surge of deep and muddy water winding its way through paddy fields, way beyond our boundaries – we might catch a snake, a poisonous one. That would serve our governess right.'

'We were ghastly children,' Margo recalled. 'We were a gang, Leslie and me, and Leslie was the gang leader. But he was very delicate and so he got a lot of attention. Anything going, he caught, all the major illnesses. Mother indulged him; I always thought he should be indulged because he was the weakest of us. But I was a toughie.'

Leslie and Gerry with their ayah.

For a while, the garden at the house in Jamshedpur was home to two Himalayan bear cubs. The cubs left an indelible impression on the infant Gerry, thanks to the antics of Leslie and Margo. The cubs were a gift from Uncle John, Louisa's brother, a big-game hunter, and though they had been weaned they had come straight out of the wild and no attempt had been made to tame them. 'They had very long sharp claws and very sharp white teeth,' Gerry remembered, 'and uttered a series of yarring cries of rage and frustration.' They were temporarily housed under a big domed basket on the rear lawn, where a servant was instructed to look after them. Gerry told the story, many years later, in an autobiographical fragment:

> Of course, having your own bears was a wonderful thing, even though they did smell very lavatorial. And, of course, at that age Margaret and Leslie were ripe for any sort of mischief. As soon as the boy detailed to look after the bears went to get some food they would overturn the basket and run screaming into the house saying, "The bears are out! The bears are out!" After two or three days of this my mother's nerves could stand no more. She was terrified that the bears would escape and find me sitting on my rug and proceed to disembowel me.

And so the bears were sent away to the zoo, reducing the family menagerie to Bindle, a cocker spaniel, and Jessica, Margo's pet duck.

* * *

Glory Dixie, the daughter of Louisa's brother John, would visit her aunt's family at Kurseong and Jamshedpur and observed their behaviour. 'Larry was always robust, a typical small boy. He was always up to pranks but he was somebody who made everything very cheerful and happy, you know. And Margo was always robust. But Leslie was totally different. I can remember Leslie holding his breath to get what he wanted and Aunt Lou would panic that Leslie would die, and Leslie would be given whatever he wanted.'

Glory recalled that Louisa and Lawrence Samuel would go to the club for a game of tennis but that otherwise she was a homebody. 'She wasn't really a social person at all, not for going out or dances. Her family meant everything to her.' Sometimes

Lawrence Samuel would go to the club without her. 'He would enter into everything. He was a good tennis player, he sang, there were fancy dress parties and amateur theatricals, and he used to take part in them all. I can remember him dressed as a Pierrot and singing a song called "Wallah Walloo". As a girl of twelve I thought how smashing he was.'

Louisa, having lost one child to diphtheria and given birth to Leslie during a cholera epidemic, kept the *Medical Annual* at her elbow and was always on the alert for snake bites, poisons, rabies, leprosy or yellow fever. 'We used to eat berries and goodness knows what,' said Margo, 'and that would drive her crazy.' Louisa would call for their local doctor 'at every possible moment', so often that he became a friend of the family. Dr Chakravati was his name, a small chubby man who would bump his old bicycle along the dirt roads, black bag in hand, to respond to Mother's pleas.

> 'What is the trouble today, dear lady?' he would say with warm concern as he came puffing up the veran-dah steps. 'Oh dear Dr Chakravati,' Louisa would say anxiously, 'Is that plant on the verandah poisonous? The children have been sucking the milky juice from its leaves,' to which Dr Chakravati would respond, 'Oh dear dear, castor oil must be given to all.'

At another summons the black bicycle bounced to a standstill, Dr Chakravati hurried into the dining room, which Louisa had converted into a spotless hospital operating theatre. It was 'goodbye tonsils' day, recalled Margo.

> 'You can rely on me, dear lady Mrs Durrell, to make a good job of it,' he said with confidence, and the tonsils were removed one by one without fuss.

And then there was the occasion when Leslie developed tropical sprue, an inflammation of the small intestine which weakens the body due to malnutrition. The cure was found only in the 1940s, but decades earlier Dr Chakravati had his own remedy. Leslie had to drink fresh chicken's blood, the chicken killed there and then because the blood had to be warm.

The prospect of castor oil and chicken's blood did not deter Leslie from feigning illness in order to get attention. Margo, his accomplice in many other ways, was sceptical when he ran a temperature.

> Should the doctor be called, or is it because his parents are having a social night at the club and he is determined to ruin their evening?

Though Margo knew that 'Leslie was so delicate', she also knew that 'he was a good actor and an expert at manufacturing high temperatures'. At the slightest hint that Leslie was unwell, Louisa would rush to him. But Margo and the governess would discuss the situation and more often than not agree that Leslie could survive the night without disturbing his parents.

There were, however, occcasions when serious medical attention was called for:

> 'Oh dear Dr Chakravati,' said Mother wringing her hands. 'Margo has been bitten by a dog, our neighbour's. Could it be mad?' Their best friends' dog had nipped Margaret as she was petting it while it was deep asleep. 'We will have to wait and see developments, dear lady,' said Dr Chakravati. Leslie hovered eagerly, or so she felt, waiting for his sister to foam at the mouth.

But when Margo was again bitten by a sleeping dog, Dr Chakravati urged that the dog be tested for rabies. This time it was Bindle, the family dog, and he had bitten Margo's face. The test had to be done at Simla, the imperial summer capital of British India high in the Himalayas, a thousand miles to the northwest of Jamshedpur. Mother, the *ayah*, the governess, various servants, and Margo and Leslie all made the two-day journey by train. Bindle went too, or at least his severed head which was carried in a canister to be tested. Margo was worried about being scarred for life, not about the possibility of being infected with rabies. She was protected by the holy water given her by the governess:

> 'From Lourdes,' she explained with holy reverence, and I, awe-inspired by her tone, kept the bottle safe for years. In fact, I recall taking it carefully wrapped in a handkerchief to England and eventually to Corfu in 1935. No one knew this secret!'

Father had remained at home where he was visited by an unexpected guest that sent the cook into a panic. Looking for something suitable for the occasion, and not realising Jemima's place in the family tree, the cook turned Margo's pet duck into a pot roast.

* * *

According to his mother, Gerry's first word was 'zoo'. The zoo was in Lahore, in the Punjab, where Lawrence Samuel moved the family in 1927, when his contract at Jamshedpur came to an end. Gerry had just turned two and long remembered that first pungent smell of leopards and tigers. He retained early sensations too of gold and yellow and scarlet sunsets, the vivid colours of saris and food in the bazaars, the smell of coriander and curries at home, the taste of his favourite breakfast, boiled rice in buffalo milk, the sound of parakeets squeaking and fluttering across a green sky.

Scent and sound and brilliant colour pervaded Gerry's memories of his first years, his earliest sensations of what he later described as this 'magical and beautiful' world into which he had been born. One day when his *ayah*, a plump motherly woman in a spotless white sari, was taking him on his daily walk, she stopped to gossip with friends, men wearing turbans and belted in green, and women swathed in saris, one of magenta embroidered with gold and silver. Gerry slipped away and wandered over to a shallow roadside ditch, where he discovered a pair of pale coffee-coloured slugs crawling over one another in a strange mad dance. He was watching in fascination as they covered one another with glistening slime when his *ayah*, discovering he was gone, raced over to the ditch in a panic. 'She immediately pulled me away and told me I must not touch or even watch such disgusting creatures. I remember at the time being puzzled because to me they were beautiful and not ugly at all.' Throughout his life Gerry would return to the colours of that day, to the gleaming slugs glistening each other with the slime of their bodies, and to the enchanting

The young naturalist: Gerry at two.

woman in the rich magenta, which forever remained one of his favourite colours.

Gerry claimed to have a photographic memory and stored impressions of animals and colours and tastes and scents, and he kept a watchful eye on his family too. Being so much younger than the others he had the advantage of being able to observe them while they hardly noticed him.

* * *

Gerry had very little memory of his father, nor of his death, which happened when he had just turned three, on 16 April 1928. But Margaret, nine years old, remembered it well.

> It was a trauma. And it was a very great trauma for Mother. People advised us to go to Dalhousie. And Dad was taken into the hospital there. But he never recovered. Father was a tall handsome man with gentle manners and much loved by all. I have missed him, his image and his strong presence all my life. How much more must Mother have grieved when we lost him.

The death of Lawrence Samuel changed everything; his driving purpose and his confident determination had set the course of their lives. The tragedy began in Lahore, in early 1928, when he began to suffer severe headaches. Friends put it down to exhaustion and suggested that he take a rest in the cool hill station of Dalhousie. The entire family moved into a rented house there, with the governess, the *ayah*, a chauffeur and other servants. But the headaches worsened and he began to behave irrationally. 'You couldn't trust him,' said Margo.

Lawrence Samuel was admitted to Dalhousie's English cottage hospital and Louisa moved in with him, leaving the children in the charge of the governess. 'The governess used to take us every day up to the hospital and we went to Mass at the Catholic church every morning. We were made to pray, more, longer prayers, louder prayers; we lit more candles, went to church more often. Frightened, we huddled close to our *ayah* and governess. Our governess had great faith in the priest who became a symbol of hope.'

Lawrence Samuel had probably been suffering from a brain tumour; the registrar entered a cerebral haemorrhage as the immediate cause of death. Margo recalled:

> Leslie and I were allowed a last farewell visit: we saw Father briefly in the long, muted white ward, a remote still body covered by a white sheet. Mother was standing on the hospital verandah to greet us. She wore a plain blue dress, an image imprinted on my memory: white-faced, stricken yet calm – her inner strength had prevailed as my childhood memory recalls. I do not remember the funeral – I can only think that we were shielded from the last ritual and the breaking up of our home.

Years later Louisa admitted that she had thought of commit-ting suicide but went on living for the sake of Gerry, three years old and entirely dependent on her. She also told Margo that she had nearly become a Catholic after being 'supported and strengthened by the presence of the Catholic nuns who daily gave her compassion, companionship and spiritual strength, which she could not find in any other religion'.

Larry was at school in England when his father died. 'Larry just got a telegram,' said Margo. 'He had no family around him. The death that is most difficult to get over is the absent death; Larry had his father at his shoulder for the rest of his life.'

'The moment my father died,' remembered Gerry, 'I was whisked away by my *ayah* to stay with nearby friends, leaving my mother, heartbroken, with the task of reorganising our lives.' India was no place for a woman to raise four children, Louisa was told by people in the English community. And so she sold the house, had everything shipped off ahead, and

Larry during schooldays in England.

taking the train to Bombay the Durrells set sail for a country they hardly knew but which they called home.

'I have a few trivial memories of our railway journey down to the coast,' Gerry said. 'At one point the train ran along the banks of a river where women were washing clothes and huge buffaloes wallowed in the shallows and small boys scrambled over their huge chocolate bodies, rubbing them with stones. I wanted to join them and help them clean the buffalo, but Mother said that there was no time. Further along the river I saw my first camel, pacing slowly and sardonically along. I dearly wanted to stop the train so that I could get on a more intimate friendly footing with this fantastic animal but Mother said there was no time.'

Chapter 2: **England**

THE FIRST VISIT THE DURRELLS ever made to England was in 1923, the year they brought Larry to start his schooling there. The family came again two years later and enrolled Leslie at Dulwich College in suburban south London, where he remained for only a year; when they returned in 1926 Louisa found that Leslie had been bullied at school and took him back to India, but not before Lawrence Samuel bought an eight-room house at 43 Alleyn Park in leafy Dulwich into which he intended they would eventually settle.

To this large empty house, 'sheltering behind a grim, dripping, choking laurel hedge', as Gerry remembered, a house empty of her husband and of her children's father, Louisa came when she arrived from India in 1928. But the empty house was haunted by ghosts.

Louisa's cousin Prudence, who everyone called Aunt Prue, was 'one of our nicest relatives', said Gerry; she had been living in England for some while and came round to help Mother settle in. Almost the first thing she said was, 'Louie, dear, you oughtn't to be living in a house like this alone – most unwise. We must get a man.' An advertisement was placed in the press and eventually Stone was hired, a polite man in his fifties who polished the silver and cooked simple meals. But unfortunately he went home in the evenings, leaving the great empty house unprotected at night.

'We must get a watchdog, Louie dear', said Prue. So, early the next morning Louisa went out and by lunchtime, according to Gerry, recounting the family story, she returned triumphantly. Sitting next to her in the taxi was one of the biggest bullmastiffs ever bred. Mother named him Prince.

At night Prince was stationed in the sitting room against anyone attempting to break in. One night, however, as Prince was being led to the room he growled menacingly, the hair on his hackles stood up, and he refused to pass through the door. Mother peered into the room but could see nothing. She switched on the lights but still there was nothing to be seen. But now Prince's attention was riveted on the big empty armchair.

Then Louisa placed Gerry just inside the darkened room. 'What do you see?' she asked. After a pause Gerry answered excitedly, 'I see my Daddy!' 'What's he doing?' Mother asked. 'He's sitting in the chair, smoking,' Gerry said, and went on to describe the smoking jacket his father always wore when he returned from work and was having his *chhota peg*, his after dinner malt whisky.

With Prince still growling furiously at the door, Mother took Gerry and Prue to the kitchen and made tea. When they went back to the drawing room, Prince entered it without complaint. Gerry saw nothing; his father was gone.

* * *

Gerry's stories of his time in Dulwich overlook the existence of his siblings. He gives the impression that the house was empty except for himself, his mother and for a while Aunt Prue; the others were away. This was probably the case, for Leslie and Margo were sent off to boarding schools around this time. Leslie, who was ten in 1928, was at some point enrolled at Caldicott Prep School in Hampshire; Margo, nine, was placed in Malvern Girls' School in Worcestershire; and Larry, sixteen,

Gerry in Dulwich, 1929.

who had left St Edmund's at the end of the previous year, was boarding at Wratting Park in Cambridgeshire, where he was being coached for the Oxford and Cambridge entrance exams, and later, until about summer 1929, attended a military-run 'crammer' to the same end. Larry probably began living in Dulwich from that time, but otherwise the family only came together at holidays; for the rest of the year Louisa and Gerry mostly spent their days alone.

The arrival and the departure of Prince bracketed the two years that Louisa would live in Dulwich. Prince, who Gerry reckoned was 'about the size of a Trafalgar Square lion', dragged Louisa and Prue from tree to tree when they took him on walks. One morning Prince pounced upon an unescorted Pekingese. Louisa and Prue screamed in horror as Prince tossed the Pekingese into the air and gave it two great chomps in his jaws and tossed it aside dead. 'I do hope he is not going to make a habit of that,' said Louisa as she and Prue revived themselves with a brandy and soda.

'Probably he did not consider them dogs', thought Gerry, 'because they were so small. He may have thought they were rats or small rabbits. Be that as it may, yells and screams from Mother and Prue, accompanied by belabouring with umbrellas and handbags, Prince merely took as encouragement.' Prince went from one small dog to another, a Pomeranian one day, a Yorkshire terrier the next, a succession of Chihuahuas and toy poodles and other small breeds in the following weeks. After paying several stiff sums in compensation, Louisa decided to retire Prince to a farm in the country, where, in Gerry's words, 'he could pick on something more his size, like a bullock'.

'I wept passionately at our parting and gave him a bag of peppermints to remember me by,' lamented Gerry, though he soon enough forgot all about Prince in the excitement of moving from Dulwich to new quarters in Upper Norwood.

* * *

In 1930 Louisa decided that the Alleyn Park house was beyond her means, and until she knew more certainly what she wanted to do she let it out and moved into a service flat at the Queen's Hotel on Church Road in Upper Norwood, a mile and a half away. The hotel, which is still there today, is a grandiose white stucco Victorian pile built specially to accommodate visitors to the Crystal Palace after it had been removed from the site of the Great Exhibition of 1851 in Hyde Park to the heights of Norwood in 1854, where it housed exhibitions, concerts, festivals, museums and schools of art and science.

The Durrells' flat was in the bowels of the hotel, a strange elongated affair, one room opening onto another. You first stepped into a large room that served as both a drawing room and a dining room; opposite this was Larry's room; then farther along was a small room where Gerry kept his toys. Beyond this were a small bathroom and a kitchen; and finally you came to Louisa's spacious bedroom. Gerry slept in his mother's room and from his bed he could look along the entire length of the flat to the front door.

In Gerry's description there were no rooms set aside for Leslie and Margo, who stayed only during term holidays; but the flat was home to Larry, who had abandoned his studies and was discovering bohemian London, writing poetry and playing piano in a jazz band.

Two ghosts inhabited the flat, one a woman whom Louisa saw standing silently smiling at the foot of her bed before fading away. A few weeks later, when Gerry's cousin Molly was visiting, she came running to the kitchen, saying, 'Auntie, Auntie, there's a strange lady in your room.' When they went to look there was nothing there, but when Molly was questioned she described exactly the appearance and costume of the woman who had appeared to Louisa.

The other ghost was invisible but made himself heard in Larry's room – which contained Lawrence Samuel's great roll-top desk that had been made of teak to his own design. When the top was opened or closed, it screeched and roared. The sudden clatter of the desk one night startled Mother, who sat up in her bed. 'Why, Larry must be in early,' she said. 'I'll go and see if he wants anything to eat.'

Drinking gin and smoking Balkan Sobranies in bed, Louisa would wait up for Larry to come in; Gerry stayed awake too, listening to his mother reading *The Wind in the Willows* to him over and over again, but also looking forward to the outrageous anecdotes of bohemian nightlife with which Larry regaled them when he got home.

Louisa went to Larry's room but he was not there. Puzzled, she returned to bed, telling Gerry, 'I could have sworn I heard that desk,' and at that same moment the desk opened and closed again. 'I experienced it myself,' said Gerry, recalling how his mother took him by the hand and walked back down the length

Queens Hotel in 1899 – photographed by the novelist Emile Zola, who lived there while in exile from France.

of the hall, listening to the constant clacking of the desk opening and closing, which became deafening as they approached,
but when she threw open the door the noise ceased as suddenly
as it began and again there was nobody there.

Gerry held to these stories of the supernatural all his life. In
his expression he would challenge anyone to doubt these early
encounters with ghosts. They bound him to his mother.

'The hotel is crowded with ghosts', Larry wrote, too. But
this is in *The Black Book*, a novel that he wrote six years later
in Corfu, which is largely set in what he calls the Regina Hotel
in Upper Norwood, 'this tomb of masonry', a microcosm of
an England inhabited by the walking dead. 'I am dying again
the little death which broods forever in the Regina Hotel: along
the mouldering corridors, the geological strata of potted ferns,
the mouse-chawed wainscoting with the deathwatch ticks.' In
Larry's hands the genteel if faded hotel became home to pros-
titutes and gigolos, degenerates and perverts, the imbecilic and
the decrepit. 'His keeper will feed him and guard the old ladies
from shameful remarks. Afterwards he will sit in the lounge,
upright, staring at the wall, as if he were being rowed down the
Styx, fighting motionless campaigns in his skull.' But above all
it is a world of cultural vacuity, what Larry called the English
Death. 'I am the average Englishman', one of Larry's characters
says. 'I have never left school and I am proud of it. I carry my
virginity and my self-satisfaction on a string round my neck.'

But for Gerry the Queens Hotel was an awakening. He
liked their new flat because it had a side entrance that opened
onto the hotel grounds with its shrubs and flowers and a pond
which was a home to snails. But it was the sparrows and the
pigeons that Gerry liked best and he wanted to have one as a
pet. Someone told him that the only way to catch birds was to
put salt on their tails, so he spent many fruitless hours stalking
birds or hiding in the bushes and falling on them as they were
feeding, a salt cellar in one hand, a paper bag to hold them
captive in the other.

One morning as he was trailing after birds he became aware of someone walking slowly by, a pretty young woman with long glossy hair, who stopped and said, 'Hello. What are you trying to do?' Gerry explained about the salt on their tails and how difficult it was. 'It looks exhausting,' she said with twinkling eyes. 'Why don't you come to my place and have something to drink to refresh you, and you can meet my gold-fish and my cat.'

After taking Tabitha to meet his mother, Gerry went round to his new friend's flat, where she introduced him to Cuthbert her black and white cat and her two goldfish, Mr Jenkins and Clara Butt. As Tabitha was boiling the kettle for tea, she sang a song which enchanted Gerry,

Is he an Aussie, is he, Lizzie?
Is he an Aussie, is he, eh?
Is it because he is an Aussie
That he makes you dizzy, Lizzie?

By the time they had finished tea, Gerry had mastered the lyrics and they joyously sang the song as a duet.

'I know lots of songs like that. I will teach them to you', Tabitha said. 'You like music, don't you?'

'Yes, my *ayah* always used to play the gramophone for me.'

'Well, I have a gramophone too, and I've got some records, and I'll teach you to dance if you like.'

Two days later Gerry was back, and Tabitha had brought out her wind-up gramophone and a pile of records, some by Harry Lauder and Jack Buchanan. They put on the Jack Buchanan record and sang along with him; it was a Charleston, so they cleared away the furniture and Tabitha taught Gerry how to dance.

'I loved the days I spent with Tabitha,' recalled Gerry. 'She was not only very sweet and kind but very funny. She taught me all sorts of songs and she taught me not only the Charleston

Leslie, Louisa and Gerry in Bournemouth.

but how to do the waltz and at times we went round and round so fast that eventually we would collapse on the sofa, she with peals of laughter and me giggling like an hysteric. These were wonderful days, only marred by the fact that occasionally a gentleman would arrive to talk business with Tabitha and so she would leave me in charge of the gramophone while she took the gentleman into the bedroom and locked the door so that they could discuss their important business.'

Then one day Louisa caught wind of the gentleman callers and forbade Gerry to go, telling him that Tabitha was too busy to have him in and out of her flat. Gerry disagreed: 'I knew she was busy because she had so many men coming to discuss business with her, but it never seemed that I interfered with the process. But Mother was adamant. I loved Tabitha very much. She was so gentle and gay, her smile engulfed you with love. She smelt gorgeous too, which was most important to me, since Mother smelt gorgeous as well. Now I mourned the fact that I could no longer waltz and Charleston and sing silly songs with the enchanting girl.'

* * *

Among the residents at the Queens Hotel were old Mrs Richardson and her daughter and granddaughter, Mrs Brown and Dorothy. All were English but they had lived for long in America and now, rather like the Durrells, they had returned to the mother country. While they were looking for somewhere permanent to settle they had taken a flat, which, like Louisa's, let onto the garden of the hotel. Here the Browns and the Durrells soon discovered one another and became close friends. Dorothy, eleven at the time, recalled that when their cat had kittens, Gerry, then five, would come to their doorstep again and again clamouring to see them. Dorothy also observed that Gerry 'was very much a mother's boy and always terribly fond of her. As far as he was concerned she could do no wrong.'

After some exploration, Mrs Brown and her mother decided to buy a house in the salubrious seaside resort of Bournemouth in southwest England. The area was ideal, they told Louisa; the sea air was bracing and the surrounding countryside beautiful. They also told her, Margo said, that 'the sun shone more there than anywhere else in England', which is not quite true but at least it rains less in Bournemouth than most other places. Moreover, along with Eastbourne and Cheltenham, Bournemouth was the preferred retirement spot of military officers and civil servants, many of whom had seen service in the Indian Army or the Indian Civil Service and who had strong ties to friends and family who remained in India. Above all, Mrs Brown told Louisa, properties there cost very much less than they did in London. Leaving Gerry in the care of Tabitha (for this happened before Mother had discovered the worst), Louisa went down to Bournemouth to see for herself.

'Needless to say, Mother's delusions of grandeur could not be confined,' Gerry recalled. In about March 1931 'we became the proud possessors of what can only be described as a mini-mansion, Berridge House, lurking in some two acres of grounds', part woodland, part orchard, a lawn on which two games of tennis could be played at once 'and a herbaceous border slightly wider than the Nile'. The house had gigantic attics, an immense cellar, a parquet-floored drawing room running the whole length from front to back, a huge dining room and kitchen and 'an incredible number of bedrooms'. When asked by someone if the house was a little large for a widow and one small boy, Louisa answered vaguely that she had to have room for her children's friends. But Leslie and Margo were away at school and, as Gerry observed, 'the fact that they never brought any friends in the holidays passed unnoticed'.

As for Larry, he briefly lived in Bournemouth until his mother tired of his habits and said, 'You can be as bohemian as you like but not in the house. I think you had better go somewhere where it doesn't show so much.' And so sometime in

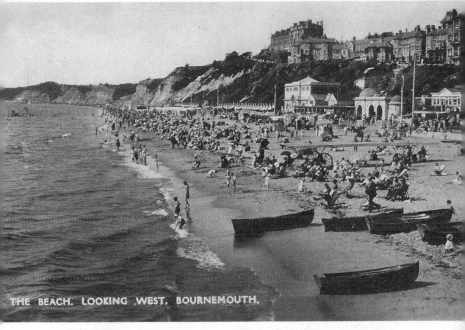

THE BEACH. LOOKING WEST. BOURNEMOUTH.

Bournemouth in the 1930s – 'a living graveyard', according to Larry.

1931 Larry began living on his own in London, working for an estate agent and collecting rents in the dismal purlieus of Leytonstone in east London by day and writing poetry by night in his room in Bloomsbury.

* * *

Gerry was too engrossed in his new environment to be aware of his mother's deteriorating condition. 'To me, the vast overgrown garden was a world to explore and delight in. To have an orchard where you picked the pink-cheeked apples and felt the sharp juice trickle down your chin, plucked ripe sun-warmed apricots from a tree that sprawled across the sunny flank of the house – fruit golden as honey, soft as velvet – all this was to me bliss.'

To celebrate moving into Berridge House Mother bought Gerry his first dog, which he named Simon, a honey-coloured cocker spaniel, a good-natured creature with limpid eyes and an overwhelming desire to please. Seeing Mother digging and weeding the herbaceous borders and hearing her bemoaning the fact that she could never get them to look like the pictures on the seed packets, Gerry's understanding was that the plants were the cause of Mother's distress and he would dig them up. But the unearthing of grasshoppers, spiders, woodlice and earwigs, which fascinated Gerry, confirmed Simon's suspicion that the world was full of evil and danger. The awful truth, as Gerry discovered, was that Simon, so admirable in many ways, was a coward. The sight of an ant or the flush of the toilet terrified him; the hissing garden hose was as deadly as a cobra; the lawn-mower was determined to pursue him and chop him up in little pieces; and when he unexpectedly came upon a snowman Gerry had made, Simon was so shocked at encountering this stranger on the lawn that he went into a nervous decline lasting days.

Simon was otherwise an amenable creature who went along with games that Gerry would invent. 'Sometimes, miraculously, he would become a pride of lions and I a lone Christian in the arena. As I prepared to strangle him, he would behave in the most un-lionlike way, slobbering over me with his moist, velvet-soft mouth and crooning endearments. Although basically a coward, he would hunt imaginary tigers or elephants with me with great skill and cunning and when our prey (my teddy bear) was captured, we would sing a rapturous duet together. I tried without success to teach him the Charleston but he could waltz fairly successfully on his hind legs if I held his front paws in an iron grip.'

* * *

Lawrence Samuel's mother, Dora Durrell, was in England in the summer of 1932 when Louisa's children were out of school and living at home; and Dora's daughter Elsie Rickwood was there too, with her husband and their two children, Molly and Phyllis. In contrast to the kindliness of Aunt Prue, who was born in Indian and on the Dixie side of the family, these paternal Durrell relations could take a harder view, disapproving of Louisa's impracticality and carelessness with money, the lack of order in her household, and the undisciplined behaviour of her children who said and did whatever they liked.

Molly recalled that 'Gerry was a beautiful little boy, really, and great fun', but that he and Leslie 'ran rings round Aunt Lou and were quite unmanageable'. Molly and her sister did not like Leslie very much. 'Leslie drove Aunt Lou mad at this time, staying in bed till midday and slouching about. He never settled to anything, never saw anything through.' And when he would sometimes condescend to play with them, 'you never knew from one minute to the next how he would behave. He would suddenly turn nasty for no reason at all'.

They were terrified by Gerry's animals but they loved it when he taught them how to ride his bicycle; they would shriek with laughter every time they fell off, until a booming voice came from on high; Larry was visiting and trying to write in an upper room from where he bellowed, 'Stop that bloody row!' Not that Gerry thought much of his two 'domineering hags of cousins' who teased and sneered and daily touted the variety and superiority of their toys to his, to which he finally replied, 'You haven't a father in heaven, but I have.'

But now with summer gone, and with it her guests and children gone away, Louisa was alone. As Gerry put it (writing as an adult): 'Incarcerated in this gigantic house with only a small boy as company, Mother took to mourning the death of my father in earnest with the aid of Demon Drink.' Louisa continued to struggle with the herbaceous borders and Gerry would join her in the kitchen as she prepared their delicious meals and tried to teach him to cook. 'But she was lonely and so she was drawn inevitably to the bottle more and more frequently.'

Gerry, at the time, noticed nothing and life went on as normal as far as he was concerned. At the end of the day he would have his bath and then climb into his mother's bed and curl up against her warm body in its silk nightgown.

And then, suddenly, one day in October 1932, Mother disappeared.

* * *

Had Gerry not written in his unpublished autobiographical jottings that his mother had had a 'nervous breakdown' and 'disappeared for a rest cure', this would have remained a secret. Louisa's breakdown is not there in *My Family and Other Animals* nor any of Gerry's other books (nor is her drinking for that matter), and Larry, Margo and Leslie never publicly brought it up. Even in his notes, Gerry says almost nothing about it, how long it lasted, how it affected him and the rest of the family. The matter was completely hushed up. 'There was only one man as far as Mother was concerned and that was Father,' Margo said. But Louisa had only a small boy and ghosts.

The secret was even more than Gerry or any of the others would admit or perhaps knew. Louisa had booked a first-class passage to India for herself and Gerry aboard the Ellerman Line's SS *City of Calcutta* sailing from Liverpool on 29 October. Her name and Gerry's are on the passenger list but were then crossed out, meaning something suddenly happened: they were about to sail but disembarked, or unexpectedly failed to board. It looks like Louisa's breakdown was an attempt to return to the land of her ghosts, to the India where she was born and where her infant daughter and her husband lay buried in the ground. Someone, possibly Larry, discovered that Louisa had decided to cut and run, and at the very last moment prevented her and Gerry from sailing with the ship.

When Louisa then entered the nursing home, or wherever it is she went, a formidable woman called Miss Burroughs moved into Berridge House to look after Gerry. 'She was not a bad woman,' he thought, when looking back on that time, but she had never looked after a small boy before and was terrified that he might wander off and get lost. 'A regime of door locking was instituted as if I were a dangerous prisoner. I was locked in the kitchen, the drawing room and the dining room, but the worst was that she banished Simon from my bedroom, saying that dogs were full of germs, and locked me in at night so that by morning my bladder was bursting and I dare not wet the bed for fear of some terrible retribution.' On top of it Miss Burroughs was a terrible cook. 'Gone were the delicious curries Mother used to concoct, gone the steaming bowls of rice like elongated pearls, chutneys like liquid amber filled with delicious fruit, gone the wonderful Indian sweets like *jalebi* oozing sugar.'

As at Dulwich, the time at Berridge House began and ended with the coming and going of a dog. Where Prince had taken to attacking other canines, it was Simon's cowardice that was his ultimate undoing. A sweep had come to clean the chimneys, carrying his rods and brushes in the sidecar of his motorbike. Simon was sleeping upstairs and was unaware of the visit; when he woke up he went down to the garden as usual to attend to nature. Just then the chimney sweep left and started up his motorbike with a terrific roar. For a moment Simon was frozen in horror; this was an even greater evil than a lawnmower or a garden hose, and in fear for his life he panicked and ran out the gate and on to the road – where Gerry watched helplessly as 'a car, unable to brake in time, neatly crushed Simon's skull, killing him instantly'.

* * *

A short time later Louisa moved again, this time to a house in Wimborne Road, much closer to the heart of Bournemouth than Parkstone. Perhaps reacting against the censure of her

Durrell in-laws, she named it for her family in Roorkee and called it Dixie Lodge.

The house and grounds at Dixie Lodge were not nearly as extensive as those of Berridge House, but it was a cosier place, while Gerry delighted in the garden, which had several highly climbable trees and inviting clusters of shrubs that were home to a variety of strange and wonderful insects. Mother found a governess for him, a raucous and benign woman called Lottie, and Gerry settled down quite happily in his new home.

'But then Mother did something so terrible that I was bereft of words. She enrolled me in the local school.' Wychwood School (which Gerry in his autobiographical notes unfailingly calls Witchwood) 'expected you to learn things like algebra and mathematics and history and, above all else, things that were anathema to me – sports.' When he played cricket, for example, a slow game which allowed Gerry a lot of time to watch the bees in the clover, he was forever missing catches, while his one achievement in football was to kick the ball into his own goal. 'We had to do a lot in gym, which meant climbing up ladders and sliding down ropes, all to no purpose as far as I could see, and then once a week a torture so monstrous that even today I shiver at the thought of it. There was a tiled room in which there was a small tiled swimming pool, and we were stripped and ranged shiveringly along the edge. Then each one of us had a huge canvas belt fitted round our waist which allowed us to be lowered into the water like a frozen bouquet garni, and instructions as to what to do with our arms and legs were shouted at us. It was sheer torture and, of course, like many of the other pupils I did not learn how to swim.' Gerry's scholastic achievements were no better; 'I was somewhat of a dullard.'

The previous year, in 1932, when Larry was twenty, he met Nancy Myers, a few months younger, who had dropped out of the Slade School of Fine Art. She was tall and slim, much taller than Larry, with light blonde hair and striking looks. Within a

Nancy Myers – who would become Larry's first wife.

The young writer – Larry in London, around 1932.

short time they were living together in Bloomsbury – Nancy had a small inheritance and Larry now had a small inheritance too from his father. In a somewhat over-flavoured account of his bohemian days in London, Larry described getting together with Nancy:

> My so called up-bringing was quite an uproar. I have always broken stable when I was unhapp ... I hymned and whored in London – playing jazz in a nightclub, composing jazz songs, working in real estate. Never really starved – but I wonder whether thin rations are not another degree of starvation – I met Nancy in an equally precarious position and we struck up an incongruous partnership ... We did a bit of drinking and dying ... Ran a photographic studio together. It crashed. Tried posters, short stories, journalism – everything short of selling our bottoms to a clergyman. I wrote a cheap novel. Sold it – well that altered things. Here was a stable profession for me to follow. Art for money's sake.

The book was his loosely autobiographical first novel *Pied Piper of Lovers*, set in India and London, which he wrote when he and Nancy, with their friends George and Pam Wilkinson, left London and went to live and paint and write in a cottage at Loxwood in Sussex for a year from mid-1933.

Nancy was an only child who had been raised in a constrained family atmosphere; part of Larry's appeal to her was that he broke all the rules. Now he began taking her down to Bournemouth, where he introduced her to his family, preparing her with sketches of what to expect: 'Larry dramatised everything – mad mother, ridiculous children, mother drunk, throwing their fortune to the winds, getting rid of everything. Hellish, foolish, stupid woman.' This, for Nancy, was a thrilling litany: 'It's wonderful to hear anybody talking about their family like that.' Nor did the Durrells disappoint. Arriving at one of those times when everyone was there, Nancy was delighted: 'Really it was the first time I'd been in a family – in a jolly family – and the first time that I'd been able to say what I liked – there was nothing forbidden to say. It was a great opening-up experience for me, hearing everybody saying, "You bloody fool!" to everybody else and getting away with it. It was marvellous. So I really fell in love with the family.'

At the first visit Mother threw Nancy and Larry out when she found them in bed together one morning, and Gerry had hopped in too. 'Out you go, out you go this minute, out you both go, five minutes and you must get out, I'm not having Gerry corrupted!' Larry brushed it off. 'Don't be such a fool, Mother.' And two weeks later they were welcomed back, Mother clucking over Nancy, trying to feed her up because she was so thin. 'And she was a marvellous cook; she did most of the cooking, a lot of hot stuff, curries, Indian cooking.'

Nancy loved what she called 'the whole craziness of it'. She recalled that 'Mother used to drink a lot of gin at that time, and she used to retire to bed when Gerry went to bed – Gerry wouldn't go to bed without her, he was afraid of being on his own, I think – and she'd take her gin bottle up with her when she went.' They would all follow her up to her bedroom and arrange themselves about her big double bed, where Louisa had an enormous silver tea tray with silver teapots and bottles on it, 'and we'd carry on the evening sitting on the bed, drinking tea and gin and chatting'. Meanwhile Gerry would happily slip into sleep. 'It was all very cosy.'

In the midst of this Larry was teaching Gerry to read, giving him children's classics like Lewis Carroll's *Alice in Wonderland*, Edward Lear's *The Owl and the Pussycat* and other nonsense poems, and A.A. Milne's *Winnie the Pooh*, which like Kenneth Grahame's *The Wind in the Willows*, so often read to him by his mother, were all tales of animals inhabiting the human world; and then there were Jerome K. Jerome's *Three Men in a Boat* and the adventure stories of R.M. Ballantyne. As

Gerry remembered, Larry's visits set everything alight: 'Larry was designed by Providence to go through life like a small, blond firework, exploding ideas in other people's minds.' His conversation was extraordinary. He could take a very ordinary event 'and by skilful embroidery, by a twist of viewpoint, and with a handful of similes, turn it into something that leaves you helpless with laughter.' And sometimes Larry would go further: 'My brother could, out of his nimble and mercurial mind, make statements which you knew to be untrue, but they were produced with such a wealth of convincing detail that you came close to believing them. And when they were hilariously comic – which they generally were – you wanted to believe them even more.'

* * *

During these visits to Bournemouth, Larry discovered a wonderful old-fashioned bookshop called Commins, which had a nineteenth-century atmosphere. A young man named Alan Thomas was in charge and decades later he would become the doyen of the British antiquarian book trade. Tens of thousands of books filled the whole of five floors and customers were free to wander at will, so little molested by pressure to buy that sometimes they were forgotten about altogether and locked in when the staff went home. Larry and Nancy would come in nearly every day, talking books and ideas and art with Alan, in whom they discovered a kindred spirit, and soon he was becoming a frequent visitor to Dixie Lodge.

'There never was more generous hospitality,' Alan recalled. 'Amid the gales of Rabelaisian laughter, the wit, Larry's songs accompanied by piano or guitar, the furious arguments and animated conversations going on far into the night, I felt that life had taken on a new dimension. Larry was writing, Nancy painting, Leslie crooning, like a devoted mother, over his collection of unlicensed firearms. Every basin in the house was unusable

Commins Bookshop, Bournemouth, and its manager Alan Thomas.

because Gerry had filled them with newts, tadpoles and such-like. Margaret, realising that book-learning was no part of her world, was rebelling about returning to school, and soon succeeded, backed by the rest of the family, in staying put.'

At the heart of it all, said Alan, was Louisa Durrell: 'it was her warm-hearted character, her amused but loving tolerance that held them together'. Many years later Gerry looked back on the family. 'It is curious – and something you don't realise at the time – but my mother allowed us to be. She worried over us, she advised us (when we asked) and the advice always ended with "but anyway, dear, you must do what you think best". It was, I suppose, a form of indoctrination, a form of guidance. She opened new doors on problems that allowed new exploration of ways in which you might – or might not – deal with them. Simple things now ingrained in me without a recollection of how they got there. I was never lectured, never scolded.'

But Larry, the eldest brother, knew it was not quite as simple as that. As much as Louisa allowed her children to grow freely, there was an unspoken understanding among them of their mother's fragility; for all their anarchy they had to look after their mother, otherwise they would have no family. Larry made a joke of it but the point was serious: 'We can be proud of the way we have brought her up; she is a credit to us.'

Chapter 3: **The Crisis**

NOT LONG AFTER GERRY HAD BEGUN at Wychwood School, Alan Thomas spotted the headmaster browsing through the shelves at Commins bookshop. He went up to him and said, 'I believe you have the son of some friends of mine at your school.'

'Oh?' said the headmaster. 'What's the name?'

'Durrell. Gerald Durrell', Alan replied.

'The most ignorant boy in the school,' snapped the headmaster and stalked out of the shop.

Gerry's rare happy moments at school came just once a week when Miss Allard, the tall blonde gym mistress, gave an hour-and-a-half class in natural history. 'She became my heroine,' said Gerry, recalling that she was the only teacher who had noticed his fascination with animals and went out of her way to foster his interests. Otherwise Gerry was a lonely and shy boy who lived in a world of improbable dreams, as when he told his mother one day, as they walked along the Bournemouth promenade, that when he grew up he wanted a zoo of his own.

School was made worse by one especially unpleasant boy who bullied pupils and then contrived to put the blame on them, so that they were sent to see the headmaster for punishment. On one occasion, Gerry recalled, the boy had been particularly obnoxious to him and he saw an opportunity to get his own back:

> whereupon his wails of distress and moans and groans had to be heard to be believed, and I was immediately told that I would have to go up to see the headmaster within the half hour.

> I went up the broad staircase into the upper part of the house and tapped timidly on the door of the great man's sanctum. He told me to come in and then gave me a lecture on bullying and how I would never get on in life if I persisted in this sort of attitude. Then he made me take down my trousers and bend over a chair. He delivered six hearty, stinging slaps to my backside and then said he hoped he wouldn't have occasion to see me up in his study again.

Fortunately this happened at the end of the day and Gerry was able to go straight home.

Christmas Greetings
FROM WYCHWOOD.

Gerry's one and only school – the dreadful Wychwood Hall.

I was flushed with embarrassment, mortification and rage. Nobody had ever lifted a finger to me, however bad my misdemeanor might have been. I half ran, half walked back home, the tears streaming down my face. I burst into the house and told the whole story to my horrified mother. I was shaking like a leaf with the indignation and unpleasantness of the whole thing. Mother wrapped me up in a blanket, put me by the fire and made me an eggnog.

'Don't you worry', she said. 'That's the last time you'll be going to that school.'

She then sat down and wrote to the headmaster saying she had no intention of keeping her son at a school where the children were flogged for misdemeanors. Larry, arriving home in the midst of this, said he thought Mother was making far too great a fuss.

'Nonsense', said Mother, 'the boy was terribly upset, and you would have been too if you'd been flogged.'

'You can't call a few slaps on the bum a flogging', said Larry. 'You're talking about it as though he had been brutalised by a cat o' nine tails'.

'Nevertheless', said Mother, 'he is not going to go back.'

And that was the end of Gerald Durrell's formal education. From the age of nine he never went to school again.

* * *

Larry's view was that Gerry was being made soft by the embrace of his mother's love. 'He never had to fight with his fists for room to breathe, as we had to in various schools and miles from home. Gerry tagged along with Ma, which was very weakening, but also very enriching. He had to struggle against the enormous indulgence granted him in living with this extraordinary mother, the most charming creature you could imagine, the most demanding in affection.'

By now Gerry had recovered from the death of Simon and Louisa decided that a new dog would help him also recover from the whole unpleasantness of school and the headmaster's beating. And so, as Gerry recalled, 'we got on one of the clanking trams and went down to the shops,' where in the window of a pet shop they saw a litter of puppies with plump bellies and black curls. 'I stood for a long time contemplating them and wondering which one I should buy. At length I decided on the smallest and the one who was getting the most bullying from the others, and who kept casting soulful glances at me from his large brown eyes. I christened him, for no particular reason, Roger.'

Roger, who grew rapidly into something resembling a small Airedale covered with the sort of curls you find on a poodle, became Gerry's stalwart companion. 'A more intelligent and brave dog I have never possessed. He was, of course, a mongrel, but to me a mongrel of pedigree.' Roger mastered several tricks such as dying for King and Country and 'now the garden became an even more exciting place for there were two of us to have adventures within it'. Roger soon recognised the Durrells as his pack, leaping to their defence, and made himself at home as one of the family – and would be made famous by Gerry and forever remembered in *My Family and Other Animals*.

'As a small boy he was impossible, a terrible nuisance,' Larry remarked. 'Of course Mother was there to defend him – the slightest criticism and she would snarl like a bear, and meanwhile there were beetles in the soup.' Alan Thomas remembered Gerry being furious with Larry, who, wanting to wash, had pulled the plug out of a basin full of marine life. 'Spluttering with ungovernable rage, almost incoherent, searching for the most damaging insult in his vocabulary: "You, you (pause), you AUTHOR, YOU"'.

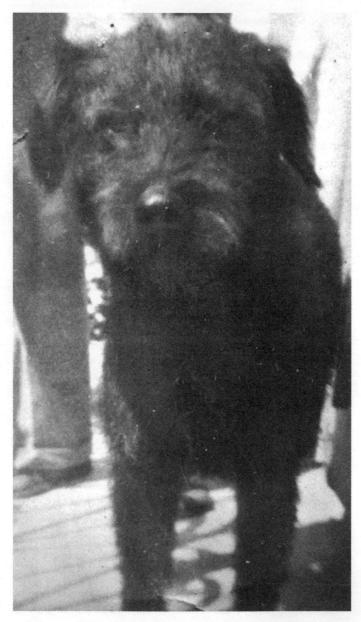

Roger – the dog who came with Gerry to Corfu.

This was at the time when Larry was living in the cottage in Sussex and writing his first novel, *Pied Piper of Lovers*. If Gerry did not appreciate Larry pulling the plug on his marine life, he was nevertheless stimulated by his brother's visits to Bournemouth, where he remembered Larry taking him to the theatre to see *The Tempest* and stimulating an interest in poetry. 'When I was just six or seven years old and Larry was a struggling and unknown writer, he would encourage me to write. Spurred on by his support, I wrote a fair bit of doggerel in those days and Larry always treated these effusions with as much respect as if they had just come from the pen of T.S. Eliot. He would always stop whatever work he was engaged upon to type my jingles out for me and so it was from Larry's typewriter that I first saw my name, as it were, in print.'

If many people today know Lawrence Durrell from Gerry's affectionate lampoon in *My Family and Other Animals*, much of the credit for Gerry's development belongs to Larry, though he always gave full dues to Gerry himself. 'Gerry has overcome this weird childhood and turned himself into a man, and a tough one, and a fully developed one, in the teeth of an upbringing that might well have justified no career at all.'

* * *

In 1934, Lottie's husband became seriously ill with cancer and reluctantly she gave up her position as Gerry's governess at Dixie Lodge to look after him. Back to square one, as Gerry put it, because as much as anything else Lottie had been a companion to Louisa, but now with the holidays over, and friends gone away and Leslie and Margo back at school, it was 'lonely evenings where Mother had only myself as company'. She returned, more seriously than ever, to 'the Demon Drink'.

Larry was still at Loxwood in Sussex with Nancy, finishing his novel. However, their friends George and Pam Wilkinson had left in June to bicycle across Europe and in September they had reached Corfu. George was writing enthusiastically to Larry about the island idyll they had discovered where life was cheap and free of pressure; they were having a boat built and were putting together a travel book. Greece seemed the answer for Larry and Nancy. Living more easily on their inheritances in Greece than in England, they could devote themselves entirely to writing and painting and travel. 'Corfu is the ideal place to use as a base for Mediterranean exploration: Nancy is rabid to examine the traces of early Byzantine painting down that coast of Greece,' Larry replied, while he was eager to get to Knossos and examine the traces of Minoan civilisation, adding that he would bring 'a huge small library' to provide 'food for study and delight'.

But then Larry learnt something that made him tear his letter open again, and now he added, 'The days are so dun and gloomy that we pant for the tropics: as much too, to see your faces again. My mother has gotten herself into a really good financial mess and has decided to cut and run for it. Being too timid to tackle foreign landscapes herself, she wants to be shown around the Mediteranean by us. She wants to scout Corfu, largely because your letters have stimulated her so.' But Larry was making excuses and covering up; Louisa had not got herself into a financial mess; when he writes of his mother cutting and running, he has in mind her heavy drinking now and her breakdown a year and a half before. Having begun his letter talking of himself and Nancy coming to Greece, he was now including the whole family.

In the opening pages of *My Family and Other Animals* Gerry gives his famous account of why the family went to Corfu, being funny as the Durrells could always be when skirting over serious things, and, like Larry's letter to George Wilkinson, an exercise in avoiding the truth.

Gerry's account begins with a cold, grey, drizzling August afternoon in Bournemouth. He is plugged up with catarrh and can barely speak or breathe; his older brother Leslie is largely deaf to the world owing to a persistent ear infection; his sister Margo is suffering a renewed attack of acne on her already blotched face; and their mother Louisa is wheezing and sneezing with a cold and is being bitten by rheumatism. 'Your family,' Larry tells her, 'looks like a series of illustrations from a medical encyclopedia'.

> 'I can't be expected to produce deathless prose in an atmosphere of gloom and eucalyptus' says Larry. 'What we need is sunshine ... a country where we can grow.'
>
> 'That would be nice,' says mother who is deep into a large volume called *Easy Recipes from Rajputana*.
>
> Larry has had a letter from George Wilkinson that morning; George says Corfu is wonderful. Why don't we pack up and go to Greece?
>
> 'Very well, dear, if you like,' says mother unguardedly. Usually careful not to commit herself to Larry's enthusiasms she realises she has made a mistake and quickly recovers herself. It would mean selling the house, she says, and I have only just bought it. Sell it anyway, while it is still fresh, says Larry.
>
> 'Don't be ridiculous dear,' says Mother, 'that would be madness.'
>
> So we sold the house and fled from the gloom of the English summer, like a flock of migrating swallows.

That is Gerry's comic version in *My Family and Other Animals*. But actually the decision to go to Corfu was taken in late autumn or winter and the family set sail before spring. And, as Gerry reveals in his autobiographical fragments, much more than climate and illness lay behind the migration to Corfu; Larry saw that Louisa was falling back into heavy drinking and, 'recognising the pitfalls that lay ahead, decided that decisive action must be taken'.

Larry was not free to go to Corfu and leave his mother behind – 'the pitfalls' included another breakdown and worse – and so if he and Nancy wanted to live their lives as artists in Greece, Larry would have to take his mother and Gerry too. Then Margo refused to stay behind at Malvern School and said, 'Well, if you're all going to Corfu, I'm coming,' and Leslie decided to leave his school (he was boarding at Pangbourne College in Berkshire) and come too. Mother did not say no. 'Corfu was an escape in a way,' said Margo, looking back on their adventure a lifetime later. As for the consequences, 'None of us gave it any serious thought.'

And so they sold the house, and all their belongings were boxed up and sent ahead to Corfu. Gerry gave his white mice to the baker as a present to his son, as he knew they would have a good home there; he gave his canary to the man next door who already had quite a collection of finches; and Billie the tortoise went to Lottie, who, twenty-seven years later, when Gerry was famous, wrote to him asking if he wanted it back. 'Then somebody said Roger would need a certificate before we could take him into Greece. This turned out to be a most complex piece of bureaucatic idiocy and eventually we got an enormous paper, done in copperplate handwriting, and ending in a huge red seal. This was Roger's passport and, needless to say, nobody ever wanted to consult it.'

* * *

In *My Family and Other Animals* Gerry gives the impression that the entire family, including Larry (but not mentioning Nancy), travelled across Europe by train before making the ferry crossing from Italy to Corfu. In fact Larry and Nancy led the way after getting married at Bournemouth on 22 January 1935, then on 2 March they set sail from the Port of London at Tilbury aboard the P&O liner SS *Oronsay* bound for Naples, from where they took the train to Brindisi and the overnight

N.Y.K. LINE
s.s. "HAKONE MARU"

The SS *Hakone Maru* in which the family set sail for Greece.

ferry to Corfu. The rest of the family followed in their wake
within a week, sailing from Tilbury on 6 March aboard the SS
Hakone Maru, a Japanese cargo boat of the NYK Line.

As the SS *Hakone Maru* fought its way across the Bay of
Biscay en route to Gibraltar, Leslie wrote to Alan Thomas: 'We
had a heavy snow storm this morning and we had to go up
to the top deck where the lifeboats are and give that *******
dog some exercise. God what a time we had, what with the
dog piddling all over the place, the snow coming down, the old
wind blowing like HELL – God what a trip! No one seemed to
know what to do at lifeboat drill, so if anything goes wrong it
will only be with the Grace of God (if there is one) if any of us
see the dear coast of Old England again.'

But, once in the Mediterranean, everything changed. In the
opening lines of *Prospero's Cell*, his book about Corfu, Larry
recounts the passage from Italy to Greece as though crossing a
magical latitude: 'Somewhere between Calabria and Corfu the
blue really begins ... You are aware of a change in the heart of
things.'

Gerry recalled the family being up on deck that morning, 'straining our eyes to see our new destination, our new home'. Compared to the muted colours of England, where sunlight seems to pass through a veil, 'in Corfu the light was so intense, so brilliant that it brought out every minute detail of land-scape, trees, creatures, the sea and the rocks. This brilliant light, of course, not only heightened the colours of everything but also the smells and scents of flowers and trees, the smell of the sea and the smell of the very earth of which the island was constructed. It was like being allowed back into Paradise. Our arrival in Corfu was like being born for the first time.'

That was the memory and that became the truth; Corfu would become a paradise for the family. But the Durrells' first encounter with Corfu was not quite like that, as their letters at the time show. They had arrived in a country whose language and ways they did not know. Louisa's bank in London had not forwarded any money, leaving them penniless and forcing them to borrow from the proprietor of their pension. Larry's and Nancy's books and baggage had not arrived, so they barely had a change of clothes. Margo and Gerry were miserable with homesickness and would hardly stop crying. And Louisa's searches for a place to live met with the discouraging discovery of a lack of plumbed-in toilets.

'Don't believe a word they say about this smelly island,' she added as a PS to a letter from Leslie to Alan Thomas. And Larry wrote despairingly of his mother to Pat Evans, a mutual friend of Larry's and Alan's: 'Like the blue fart that she is, she says the heat is too much, the flies too many, and the Greeks too insanitary. I'm afraid she might go back any day. What a waste of money!'

Chapter 4: **Corfu – the Strawberry-Pink Villa**

'THE FAMILY CRAWLED ASHORE TODAY,' Larry wrote to Alan Thomas from Corfu. Larry and Nancy had arrived not much earlier; they had been delayed at Brindisi for several days. In *My Family and Other Animals*, however, Gerry describes the entire family arriving together (though as always he excludes Nancy), with Mother leading the way, 'looking like a tiny, harrassed missionary in an uprising' and being 'dragged unwillingly to the nearest lamp post by an exuberant Roger and forced to stand there, staring into space, while he relieved the pent-up feelings that had accumulated in his kennel'.

From the port Louisa and her family took a horsedrawn cab to the Pension Suisse and 'took us in bed so to speak,' as Larry put it. The family also brought the news that the publishers Cassell in London had offered to publish Larry's first novel, *Pied Piper of Lovers*, marking the beginning of a career that would lead through *The Alexandria Quartet* and *The Avignon Quintet*, with several island books along the way, starting with *Prospero's Cell*, the book he would write about Corfu.

The Pension Suisse was in Moustoxidou Street, lined with handsome buildings, among them several Venetian mansions. The Dimomitsi Mansion is today the Serbian Museum, while next door stands the seventeenth-century Ricci Mansion, an arcade running across its façade, the keystones of its arches adorned with sculpted female and male heads. This was then the Pension Suisse, where the Durrells had rooms with a small balcony overlooking the street. Below them in Venetian times the nobility and dignitaries of the town would gather on the large balcony that ran atop the arcade to watch the jousting

This Corfu street scene was taken by one of the Durrells from the balcony of the Pension Suisse. From here the Durrells set off in Spiro's big car to find a villa ('with bathrooms').

contests on the last Thursday of Carnival, the most important event of the Corfiot year. The Germans bombed Corfu during the Second World War and hit the Pension Suisse (which moved to a building in the Liston overlooking the Esplanade, the town's great central square, that some mistakenly identify with the pension known to the Durrells). In Moustoxidou Street, the façade of the Ricci Mansion has since been restored; however, the interior is different to what it was when the Durrells were here.

Venice had ruled Corfu since 1386, when it became a major bulwark against the expansion of Islam. The island was the only part of Greece never to be occupied by the Ottoman Turks after they conquered Constantinople, the capital of the Byzantine Empire, in 1453 – as late as 1913, the Turks stood on the mainland just two miles across the straits from Corfu. Venice's generally benevolent and serene dominion lasted four centuries and deeply affected the architecture, landscape, culture, cuisine and prosperity of the island. The shady woods of olive trees which clothe the undulating hillsides and valleys were a Venetian planting scheme; the island possessed a nobility who wore Venetian titles and whose Venetian mansions adorned the countryside and the town; and until the mid-nineteenth century Italian was the lingua franca in Corfu. Napoleon seized the island when he extinguished the Venetian Empire in 1797, but after the Battle of Waterloo in 1815 he was relieved of it by the British, who established a protectorate over Corfu and the other Ionian Islands. However, despite centuries of foreign domination, they had never ceased to feel Greek, and in 1864 the British united them with a recently independent Greece, an act that long contributed to the warm feelings of the Corfiots towards the English.

Gerry was sensitive to the Venetian presence, describing in *Birds, Beasts and Relatives* 'the facades of tall, elderly Venetian houses of the town, crumbling gently, coloured in pale shades of cream and brown and white and cyclamen pink'. But no romance attached to Louisa's first impressions; not only was Corfu Town smelly, it was also a death trap. Margo remembered that, from their balcony at the Pension Suisse, 'we saw a lot of funerals passing, and Mother was very alarmed because she thought there must be an epidemic of something. Mother was plagued by visions of epidemics.'

As Gerry explains in *My Family and Other Animals*, 'It was unfortunate for Mother's peace of mind that the Pension Suisse happened to be situated in the road leading to the local cemetery.'

> As we sat on our small balcony overhanging the street an apparently endless succession of funerals passed beneath us. 'I'm sure it's an epidemic,' she exclaimed at last, peering down nervously into the street.

ΛΙΣΤΟΝ ΚΕΡΚΥΡΑΣ — LISTON CORFOU

Corfu Town: the Liston, with the Esplanade on the right. The arcaded building on the left is the one the Pension Suisse moved into after it was bombed out. It was here that the taxi ranks would have been – and where Spiro made his appearance into the Durrells' lives.

'Nonsense, Mother; don't fuss,' said Larry airily.

'But, dear, so *many* of them. It's unnatural. I'm sure it's something to do with the drains. There's nothing for it. We'll have to move. We must get out of town. We must find a house in the country at *once*.'

* * *

The next morning, as Gerry tells it, Louisa set off with the hotel guide who drove her here and there about the island and showed her ten villas, but always Mother said no – not one had a bathroom. Somewhere in Corfu there must be a villa with an internal bathroom and toilet and she was determined to find it, so on the following day Louisa took the family to the taxi rank in the square, where 'perceiving our innocent appearance' the drivers leapt from their cars and advanced on them like vultures. Their eyes flashed, their voices grew louder, 'and then they laid hold of us as though they would tear us apart', though, as Gerry later realised, 'we were being treated to the mildest of mild altercations, but we were not used to the Greek temperament'.

Leslie was threatening to poke his assailants in the eye, Margo was yelling 'We English, we no understand Greek', and Mother, who was fighting to escape the clutches of a driver hustling her towards his car, called out to Larry, 'Can't you *do* something', when suddenly a great rumbling voice reduced everyone to silence, 'the sort of voice you would expect a volcano to have'.

'Hoy!' roared the voice. 'Yous wants someones who can talks your own language. Thems bastards, if yous will excuses the words, would swindles their own mothers. Excuses me a minute and I'll fix thems.' Nearly knocking the drivers off their feet with ferocious imprecations in Greek, he turned to the Durrells and asked them, 'Wheres you wants to go?'

'We are looking', said Mother, 'for a villa with a bathroom. Do you know of one?'

'Bathrooms? Yous wants bathrooms? Sure, I'll takes you,' he said as he waved them into his Dodge open touring car. Off they shot, honking and twisting through the narrow streets, swerving in and out of carts and donkeys and peasant women, and out into the country, the car swooping wildly from one side of the road to the other as he turned his head to talk to the family.

'Yous English? Thought so. English always wants bathrooms. Spiro's my name, Spiro Halikiopoulos, they alls calls me Spiro Americano on accounts of I lives in America. Yes, spent eight years in Chicago. That's where I learnt my goods English.' After eight years Spiro had made enough money to return to Corfu and brought the Dodge, 'best ons the islands, no one gets a car like this'.

Careering down the narrow winding coast road south of Corfu Town, Spiro kept up the chatter, reassuring them that all the English liked him, 'they knows they won't be swindled. I likes the English. Best kinds of peoples. Honest to Gods, ifs I wasn't Greek I'd likes to be English.'

Dipping up and down against the backdrop of the Aya Deka range, passing cottages and gardens and patches of wild strawberries, the great Dodge reached Perama, six miles south of town, and roared up a hill covered in olive trees, where Spiro jammed on the brakes. 'Theres you ares, thats the villa with the bathrooms, likes you wanted.'

Behind them the sea sparkled. Pontikonisi ('Mouse Island') floated beneath them, while on the gentle rise before them, set amidst cypress trees, its creamy green shutters faded by the sun, was a small pink villa blinking in the light, awakening in an overgrown garden blooming with flaming red roses, others

Spiro in his taxi, with Margo, Gerry and Louisa in the back, probably photographed by Leslie, who took most of the family photographs in Corfu.

delicately moon-white, luxuriant bougainvillaea and bright marigolds. 'As soon as we saw it', writes Gerry, 'we wanted to live there; it was as though the villa had been standing there waiting for our arrival. We felt we had come home.'

* * *

The villa had no name. It was simply home. Afterwards the family would call it the first villa. Only when Gerry wrote *My Family and Other Animals*, twenty years later, did he give it the name of the Strawberry-Pink Villa. Built in 1931 as a rental property by the owner of the Pension Suisse, it was arranged as a square with three large bedrooms and a kitchen off a central hallway. It had a washroom and an outdoor toilet, not a proper bathroom. But that was good enough and Louisa took a six-month lease, a trial to see if she and the family liked Corfu and wanted to stay. Margo, who would turn sixteen in May, and eighteen-year-old Leslie each had a bedroom, while ten-year-old Gerry slept as he had always done in his mother's bedroom.

(The villa still remains in Perama but it is so altered that only the original footprint remains. Even the gable roof is an alteration – originally it was a flat terrace with a balustrade running round its four sides – while the Victorian garden, with its beds laid out in complicated geometric patterns of stars, half-moons, triangles and circles, has been covered by a stone terrace with a swimming pool. Today, too, the hillside is largely built up; a paved road leads there from just south of the Aegli Hotel on the coast road.)

The family had found their first home in Corfu but also they had found Spiro, or he had found them. He knew everyone, he knew how things were done, and if anyone caused trouble, 'I fixes thems.' From the day of their arrival at the Strawberry-Pink Villa, Spiro took complete control over the family's affairs. He berated the bank manager for the late arrival of Mother's funds from England; he wrested the family's luggage from the overzealous customs officials; he took them shopping in town and bargained fiercely over every drachma on their behalf; and he kept them regularly provided with fresh food – 'We ate what Spiro brought us from the market,' Margo said. The Durrells trusted Spiro completely and he remained devoted to them throughout their years in Corfu. Or, as Gerry put it, in *My Family and Other Animals*: 'Donts you worries yourselfs about anythings, Mrs Durrells, leaves everythings to me.'

Gradually the family settled in and adjusted themselves to the sometimes primitive conditions of their new island home – made easier because they had brought so little with them that their rooms were almost bare. Corfu was largely untouched by modern development. To the Venetian impress the English added schools, bridges, a postal service and some good roads extending from the town, though not too far – longer-distance travel was better done along the coast by boat. Perama was close enough to get a variety of fresh food from Corfu Town, but even so the range was limited. There was no fresh butter on the island (it came in tins) and the milk was from goats.

Spiro Halikiopoulos, photographed by one of the Durrells in Corfu.

Beef was nonexistent, chickens were scrawny, pork you had to search for, but lamb was plentiful and good. Heating depended on the charcoal fire in the kitchen or from oil heaters and wood fires in the bedrooms. For lighting, the family used paraffin with its peculiar smell.

Their first spring was unusually cold and grey, remembered Nancy, and disheartening. But as the weather got warmer the lack of refrigeration was solved by filling the ice box with blocks of ice that Spiro brought from town, 'though the best refrigerator I know', recalled Larry, 'is a deep well; and for most of my island life we lowered our bottles and tinned butter down the well in a basket with a long length of line'.

In the kitchen, Margo remembered, Mother introduced local ingredients to her curries and 'adapted to the Greek style'. But what Louisa never really adapted to was the Greek language, with unfortunate consequences, as on the occasion she had spent all morning making a special soup. 'The dialogue at lunch', wrote Gerry in his memoirs, 'went something like this':

Larry: I thought we were going to have that delicious soup for lunch.

Mother (flustered): We were, dear, but unfortunately it got ... er ... thrown out.

Larry: Thrown out?

Mother: Yes dear. Katarina threw it out of the window.

Larry (staring at her in disbelief): Why? Is the girl mad?

Mother: No, no. It's not really her fault. I gave her the soup and told her to bring it in here. I said 'Exo, to soupa'.

Larry (in exasperation): Really, Mother, you're impossible. Don't you know that 'Exo' means 'Throw it out'?

Mother (with dignity): I know it now, dear.

In another fragment of Gerry's unpublished memoirs, he reflected on the strange properties of Corfu and his childhood there:

In those days I lived a curious sort of triple life, which I was totally unaware of, and only looking back on it now do I realise how very curious it was. To begin with, I dwelt in three worlds. One was my family, one was our eccentric friends, and the third was the peasant community. Through these three worlds, I passed unobserved but observing and learning, not knowing that I was doing either, but greatly enjoying the process.

In fact everyone was eccentric: 'My family has always shown symptoms of flamboyant idiocy as far back as I can remember, so Corfu was the ideal greenhouse to bring this to full fruition.

The Strawberry-Pink Villa by Gerry. The drawing was made from memory, some time after publication of *My Family and Other Animals*, in the 1950s.

The whole atmosphere of the island and the people them-selves encouraged the eccentric in one to emerge and spread its wings.' Though Gerry does not mention it in his *Corfu Trilogy*, he knew a man who kept the elegant skull of his former mistress on his desk – bequeathed to him by her. And he knew an enchanting lady who collected empty tin cans which she kept in a Red Indian canoe hung from the ceiling in her room.

For both Gerry and Larry, the eccentric, the strange, the marvellous were aspects of the enchantment they discovered in Corfu, a place magical, where spirits mingle with mortals. Larry opens *Prospero's Cell* with a quotation from Shakespeare's *The Tempest*: 'No tongue: all eyes: be silent', the words spoken by Prospero as he invokes the spirits. (There was a nineteenth-century tradition associating *The Tempest* with Corfu, which Larry adopted with enthusiasm.) For Gerry the magic of Corfu began at the Strawberry-Pink Villa, and it began with the immense and improbable figure of Spiro Americanos/ Halikiopoulos; and it continued with other eccentric but no less real characters. There was the Rose-Beetle Man; and George Wilkinson, Gerry's tutor; and during that same first summer Dr Theodore Stephanides.

* * *

For Gerry the garden of the Strawberry-Pink Villa was 'a magic land, a forest of flowers through which roamed creatures I had never seen before'. At first he was so bewildered by the profusion of life that he went about in a daze, his attention drawn to one creature, then distracted by another, from spiders and caterpillars to flights of butterflies. 'He had an enormous patience', recalled Nancy. He would spend hours crouching or lying on his belly, looking into creatures' private lives, while Roger, gasping a sigh of resignation, flopped down nearby. 'In this way I learnt a lot of fascinating things.'

From this garden Gerry and Roger set off on their adventures. Though the house has changed and the garden has been paved over, the old pathways followed by Gerry can still be followed down to the Halikiopoulou Lagoon in one direction and through the olive groves in the other, emerging on the coast opposite Pontikonisi, Mouse Island. The landscape remains beautiful even though the ubroken groves of olives are gone, the airport lurks behind, and tourists now fill the small beaches where Gerry and Roger once ventured alone.

These were the times when Gerry first heard the haunting music of the old peasant songs, taught to him by Agathi, a woman in her seventies, who would leave off spinning wool when he appeared and have him sit with her eating grapes or pomegranates in the sun. There was the love song they would sing together called *Falsehood*, rolling their eyes adoringly at one another, Agathi trembling with emotion, clasping her hands to her great breasts. In his memoir Gerry writes the

Gerry exploring Corfu with Roger. Note the Wellington boots, insisted
upon by mother in case of snakes.

THE DURRELLS OF CORFU

lyrics in Greek and gives a translation, though in *My Family and Other Animals* he leaves out the last line.

> *Lies, lies.*
> *It is my fault for teaching you*
> *To walk around the countryside*
> *Saying that I love you.*
> *If I had loved you, you would have driven me crazy*
> *And our marriage would have been bitter.*

'What fools we are,' Gerry remembers Agathi saying to him, 'sitting here in the sun and singing of love. I am too old for it and you are too young. Ah, well, let's have a glass of wine, eh?'

One day on his travels Gerry met the Rose-Beetle Man, a weird and fascinating figure who gave all the appearance of having stepped straight out of a fairy tale. Tall and thin, wearing a long coat patched in many colours, he was a pedlar whose pockets bulged with combs and balloons and coloured pictures of the saints, while on his back he carried bamboo cages full of pigeons and young chickens, several mysterious sacks and a bundle of fresh leeks. On his head he wore a battered and floppy broad-brimmed hat stained with wine, burnt by cigarettes and smeared with dust; feathers of owls, hoopoes and cocks fluttered from the band around its crown and a great white feather that may have come from a swan.

He heralded his approach by playing on his flute, but up close Gerry noticed that his eyes were dim and had a vacant look as though blind with cataracts, and he answered Gerry's greetings with only grunts and squeaks. Gerry suddenly realised that he was mute but they continued their conversation by making pantomime gestures in the middle of the road. Strangest of all were the rose-beetles flying in circles about his head: they were tied by threads of cotton to his hat or he launched them from his hands. He sold them to children as whirling, buzzing model aeroplanes.

The Rose-Beetle Man – another remembered drawing by the adult Gerry,
for a special edition of *My Family and Other Animals* in the 1960s.

On another day the Rose-Beetle Man revealed the mystery
in one of his sacks: it was filled with tortoises. Gerry bought
one, took it home and named it Achilles; its weak spot proved
not to be its heel but its passion for strawberries, which led him
to topple down a well, a tragedy marked by Larry, who wrote
and delivered in a trembling voice a suitable funeral oration.
The Rose-Beetle Man also sold Gerry a pigeon, so repulsive
and obese that Larry suggested they name it Quasimodo. Not
that Quasimodo thought he was a pigeon; he never left the
house, walked everywhere and refused to fly, enjoyed listening
to Larry's gramophone, dancing to waltzes and marches, and
at night he slept in Margo's bed. But then one day Quasimodo
laid an egg – he turned out to be a she, and gave herself over
to a cooing admirer, who coaxed her to his tree and then they
were gone.

The Rose-Beetle Man would pass by the villa from time to time, stocking Gerry's growing menagerie with a frog or a sparrow, but the sight of all those tethered rose-beetles so distressed Gerry and Mother that in a 'fit of extravagant sentimentalism' they bought up his entire stock and released them into the garden – from where they made their way into the house: 'For days the villa was full of rose-beetles, crawling on the beds, lurking in the bathroom, banging against the light at night, and falling like emeralds into our laps.'

* * *

The family despaired of Gerry's consuming interest in animals. 'He's been in this phase since the age of two', said Mother, 'and he's showing no signs of growing out of it.' But where to find a tutor on the island? It was Larry who, though least in favour of putting Gerry through any kind of formal education, came up with the solution – his friend George Wilkinson, whose letters had drawn Larry to Corfu and who now lived with his wife Pam, also in Perama, in the Villa Agazini not far from the Strawberry-Pink Villa.

What Gerry does not say in *My Family and Other Animals* is that, when the family left the Hotel Suisse, Larry did not join them at the Strawberry-Pink Villa; instead he and Nancy took a small two-room hut close by the Wilkinsons. From there he wrote to Alan Thomas:

> I'd like to tell you how many million smells and sounds and colours this place is, but my stock of superlatives would give out. As I sit, for instance. Window. Light. Blue grey. Two baby cypresses lulling very slightly in the sirocco. Pointed and perky like girls' breasts.

Larry was happy. But he did keep an eye on things at the Strawberry-Pink Villa and in particular maintained a special responsibility for Gerry's education, though that could take

Gerry with the beginnings of his menagerie at the Durrells' first villa. He is holding Quasimodo, the obese pigeon, in his left hand, while on his lap is Achilles the tortoise – both of them acquired from the Rose-Beetle Man.

unorthodox forms, as when he started him on reading the bawdy writings of Rabelais.

'All the boys were forced into schools really,' recalled Margo, 'and they all objected to it.' But Corfu, which she called an escape, gave Leslie 'a liberty, a spiritual liberty, to get around and do what he wanted to do. He always had a gun on his shoulder, and would go out and shoot this and that and something else. He was mad about guns. Leslie was great, a card, a lovable rogue. He integrated like I did with the local scene,

Leslie in his Corfu police uniform, gun at the ready, out 'on patrol'.

and he used to go with the Condos family papa out in a police-man's uniform and check the countryside, and no doubt arrest people who were poaching a rabbit or something like that.'

But Mother was adamant that her youngest should receive a proper education and she leapt at Larry's suggestion that George be Gerry's tutor. '*That's* a brainwave. Will you go over and see him? I think the sooner he starts the better.' The following morning when George and Gerry were introduced, 'we regarded each other with suspicion'. Gerry noted his pointed

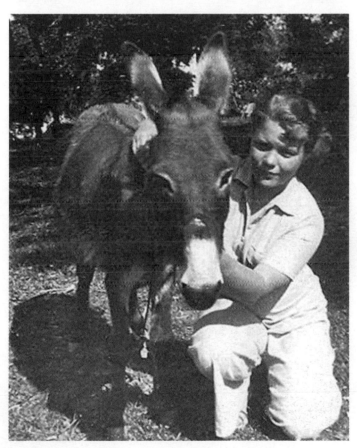

Margo, aged around fifteen, shortly after arriving in Corfu.

George Wilkinson tutoring – and fencing – by Gerry. Another drawing
from the special edition of *My Family and Other Animals*.

brown beard and large tortoiseshell eyeglasses; he was very tall
and extremely thin and moved awkwardy like a disjointed pup-
pet. Thereafter at nine each morning he would come stalking
through the olive trees in shorts and sandals and an enormous
straw hat with a frayed brim, swinging a walking stick, and
carrying a clutch of books under one arm.

George found that he could get more out of Gerry if he
introduced animals into every possible situation. This worked
well enough in geography, where maps of deserts were illustrated with camel humps, Australia was decorated with sheep
and kangaroos, and tangled jungles were home to Gerry's
drawings of jaguars and gorillas and snakes. Gerry took
to history in the same way: when studying about Hannibal
crossing the Alps, Gerry knew the name of every elephant,
just as he knew the first words of Christopher Columbus
when he discovered the New World – 'Great heavens, look, a
jaguar.' George tried the same technique with mathematics.
Instead of asking how long it would take six men to build

a wall if three could build it in a week, George would ask how long it would take four caterpillars to eat eight leaves if it took a week for two. But no number of caterpillars made mathematics comprehensible to Gerry, nor was it made easier that, as he agonised over the caterpillar problem, George was leaping and lunging round the dining room practising fencing with his walking stick or practising Greek country dancing, for which he had a passion.

For Gerry the most important hours were those devoted to natural history, when he and George would walk down to the beach and look at fishes and crabs and slugs, and George would tell Gerry all about the Battle of Trafalgar and how calm Nelson was throughout, instilling confidence in his sailors when they saw him on the bridge labelling his birds' egg collection. But, above all else, George's great contribution to Gerry's development was to teach him how to keep a diary and record his observations in a notebook: 'At once my enthusiastic but haphazard interest in nature became focused, for I found that by writing things down I could learn and remember much more.'

* * *

Whether out of boredom with his lessons or given stimulus by George, Gerry resumed writing, as he had done in Bournemouth, now producing his first extended work in prose, which he called 'The Man of Animals'. Here the ten-year-old boy sees himself as the man he will become, and not only a man of animals but a vivid and dramatic writer, the sort of boy who might one day write *My Family and Other Animals*. An interesting detail is the appearance of the cobra; as Gerry would have known, a cobra played a central part in Larry's first novel, *Pied Piper of Lovers*, which had just been published, but there the man is the enemy of the natural and traditional world and the cobra rears up, spreads his hood, and kills him. In 'The

THE man of Animals

Right in the Hart of the African Jungel
a Small wite man Lives, now there is one
grather xtrordenry fackt about Him that is
that He is the frind of **all** Animals.
now He lives on Hearbs and Bearis Both
of wich He nos, and soemtimes, not
unless He is prakticly Starvying, he shood
with a bow and arrow, a Bird of Some Sort
for you see He dos not like killing His
frinds even wene He is so week that
He cann Hardly walk.!
one of His farveret pets is a Big
gray baboon wich He named "sotine".
now there are gurten words this Big
crether nows, for intenes if His master
was to say "Sotine I want a stick to
mack a Bow* will you get me one?
then the Big king with a nod of His
Hede would trot of into the Jangel
to get a bamboo for the Bow and Arrow
But befor bracking it He would Bend
it so as to now that it would Be
all right then Breacking it of He
would trot Back to His master
And give it to Him and wight for
prase, and neddes to say His
your name out an dam faw

Gerry's earliest surviving story, 'The Man of Animals', written aged ten,
when the Durrells were living at the Strawberry-Pink Villa.

Man of Animals', however, the young man, like the old man, freely passes through the jungle as the friend of all animals – though if you have to kill, feather, gut and eat a toucan to feed yourself, that too is the way of the natural world. Gerry was not a sentimentalist.

Right in the Hart of the Africn Jungel a small wite man lives. Now there is one rather xtrordenry fackt about Him that is that he is the frind of <u>all</u> animals. Now he lives on Hearbs and Bearis Both of Which he nos, and soemtimes, not unles he is prakticly starvying, he shoot with, a bow and arrow, a Bird of some sort, for you see he dos not like killing His frinds even wene He is so week that He cann hardly walk!

One of his farveret pets is a Big gray baboon, wich he named 'Sotine'. Now there are surten words this Big crether nows, for intenes if His master was to say 'Sotine I want a stick to mack a <u>Bow</u>, will you get me one?' then the Big ting with a nod of His Hede would trot of into the Jungel to get a bamboo fo the Bow and Arrow. But before bracking it he would Bend it so as to now that it would Be all right, then Breacking it of He would trot Back to his master and give it to Him and wight for prase, and nedless to say His master would give him a lot.

The story then continues but it is told in the first person by an adventurous young man in whom Gerry would have seen himself.

One day wile I was warking in front of my porters in africa a Huge Hariy Hand caught my sholder and another one coved my mouth and I was dragged of into the Jungel by this unseen figer.

At larst I was put down (not to gently) and I found my self looking into the eyes of a great baboon. "Holy mackralel" I egeackted "what the devel made you carry me of like thish ay?' I saw the Babon start at my words and then it walked over to the ege of the clearing bekining me with a big Hairy Hand.

"Now where do you want me to go?" I arksed sur-spishely as I foleard him down a little parth. He said notheing but a little grunt of reliefe as I folled Him.

Suddenly a huge crober glied out at the side of the parth. It saw us and flatend it hade reddy to strik But the Baboon said something to it and insted of Bighting us as I had exped it to it glied towards me and twind itself about my boody and stade there, wile I (keeping my face a good way away) flooed the baboon who by thish time I had a surten faith in.

Soon we came to a little clearing in the jungel and there was a little rush hut right in the middell, to this the Baboon trooted and I floed somewhat Bewileder.

At the dore the baboon stoped and then it knoked thre times on it then a voice saide "come in Sotine". It was a verry week voice that souned as though someone was very ill.

The Baboon opened the Dore and went in I foloed and closed the dore Behind me.

And there on a bed made of Bamboos was liying a an old wite heaired man and I could see at a glance that he was very ill and why he was ill was becose he was in need of food and water. So, bring my pistol out of my houlster I went out side and shot a "Tookn" and brought it in and fatherd and guted it and then mai-king some rich soup gave the old man some after that he seemd to buck up a bit and then he said "I am very gratful to you and "Sotine" for saveing my life my Boy"

"Well now I must go" I said. "Good bye sir"

"Good by" he said.

And as I left the hut 'Sotine' gave a little wimpring cry and ran after me and gave me a big (rather wet) kiss on my cheek and ran back into the hut.

Another time I was in Afric I manged to find my way to the hut and was gratly welkumed by an old man and a big Baboon.

* * *

The way Gerry tells it in *My Family and Other Animals*, he and Roger were returning from a visit to Yani and Aphrodite. Yani was saying that he should have taken his goats to Gastouri that morning but it was too hot, so he went instead and tasted Taki's new white wine. 'Spiridion!' cried Yani, invoking the island saint, 'What a wine!' Then Yani came home and had only now awoken from an afternoon's sleep. Reaching in his pocket he pulled out a little bottle filled with olive oil, saying to Gerry, 'Here, you are interested in the little ones of God, look at this that I caught this morning, crouching under a rock like the devil.' In the bottle was a scorpion, the poison in its body seeping into the oil.

Aphrodite brought some olives and bread and figs and wine, and Yani continued. He had known a young man once, a shepherd like himself, who was returning from a fiesta warm with wine and fell asleep under a myrtle, where a scorpion crawled into his ear and when he awoke it stung him. 'Phut! Like that.' Screaming in agony the man had tried to run for his village. He never made it. They found him the next morning as they were going to the fields. 'What a sight! What a sight! With that one little bite his head had swollen up as though his brains were pregnant and he was dead, quite dead.'

That is why he always carried such a bottle, Yani explained to Gerry. 'You do not know, little lord, though you spend all your time on your stomach catching such things, eh?' he said.

'Let the sweet oil soak up the poison. Then should you ever be stung by one of his brothers (and Saint Spiridion protect you from that), you must rub the place with that oil.'

So on their way home Gerry and Roger sat down on a mossy bank and shared a gift of grapes from Aphrodite. While watching a grasshopper, a snail, a mite, pursuing their lives in their microscopic world at his feet, Gerry noticed something curious, several faint circular marks in the velvety surface of the moss. Prodding at one the whole circle opened like a trap door. Indeed it was a trap door with a bevelled edge which fitted neatly into a silk-lined shaft to which it was attached by a silken hinge. For a long time Gerry stared into this fantastic home trying to imagine what kind of mysterious creature had

View from Canoni towards Perama. In the foreground is the monastery island connected to Canoni by a causeway. The farther island is Pontikonisi (Mouse Island). This photo was taken by Leslie when the Durrells were living at the Strawberry-Pink Villa in Perama.

made it. Feeling he needed to find out immediately, he called Roger and they ran to ask George.

Out of breath and bursting with excitement, Gerry dashed through the door and only then realised that George was not alone. With him was a bearded man whom Gerry took to be his brother. Apologising for the intrusion he told George about the strange circular homes he had found.

'Thank heavens, you're here, Theodore,' said George to his guest. 'I shall now be able to hand the problem over to expert hands. Gerry, this is Doctor Theodore Stephanides. He is an expert on practically everything you care to mention. And what you don't mention, he does. He, like you, is an eccentric nature lover. Theodore, this is Gerry Durrell.'

Together they walked up the stony goat path to the olive grove, where Gerry pointed out the trap door. Delicately opening the door with the point of his pocket knife, Theodore peered in.

'Um, yes,' he said, 'They are the burrows of the trapdoor spiders, of the females of course' and he explained how she would pop out to grab and devour an unsuspecting insect, though he often wondered how the female recognised passing male spiders and did not devour them by mistake. 'He may make some sort of ... you know ... some sort of sound which the female recognises.'

Walking in silence back down the hill they shook hands and said goodbye. 'I have enjoyed meeting you,' Theodore said. As Gerry watched him strolling back towards town, he felt something important and special had happened; not only was Theodore the first person he had met who shared his enthusiasm for zoology, but he did not speak down to him; instead he treated him as an equal in age and knowledge.

'I expect we shall meet again', said Theodore at their parting.

Two days later, Gerry received a parcel with a letter inside.

My dear Gerald Durrell,

I wondered, after our conversation the other day, if it might not assist your investigations of the local natural history to have some form of magnifying instrument. I am therefore sending you this pocket microscope, in the hope that it will be of some use to you. It is, of course, not of very high magnification, but you will find it sufficient for field work.

With best wishes,

Yours sincerely,

Theo. Stephanides

P.S. If you have nothing better to do on Thursday, perhaps you would care to come to tea, and I could show you some of my microscope slides.

Chapter 5: **The Daffodil-Yellow Villa**

GERRY'S ACCOUNT OF BURSTING into George's villa and suddenly being introduced to Theodore Stephanides is a kind of shorthand – it compresses events and gets straight to what mattered to an eager ten-year old boy. At some point, maybe even on that first day, Gerry collared Theodore about the mysterious circles and as they peered into the homes of the trapdoor spiders they began to discover one another.

But Theodore's recollection of meeting the Durrells began in a more roundabout way, in a late autumn afternoon in 1934 when he was in the olive woods hunting mushrooms, and 'I suddenly came upon a thin and very tall young man with a short dark-brown beard and a very pleasant face'. The young man was George Wilkinson; they fell into conversation, quickly struck up a friendship, and walked to George's villa for tea. There George and his wife Pamela spoke of their friends Larry and Nancy, with whom they had shared a cottage for a year in Sussex and were hoping to persuade to come and live in Corfu.

And so it turned out. Early in the summer of 1935 George and Pam invited Theodore for lunch at their home, the Villa Agazini, and afterwards they walked to the Strawberry-Pink Villa nearby for tea. 'I was introduced to the Durrell clan, which included old Mrs Louisa Durrell, Leslie, Margaret and Gerald; also Roger, a large and friendly black dog of rather uncertain pedigree.' Larry and Nancy turned up soon after.

> What first struck me on meeting Lawrence was his jauntiness and self-assurance; also his bubbling energy. He seemed to be in every corner of the little house at once, throwing off advice and suggestions like a machine gun and arranging to undertake everything from the arrangement of the furniture to the planting of the garden.
>
> It was this abounding energy and self-assurance which always seemed to me the keynote of Lawrence's character. From the very beginning he was determined to become a great writer. He was quite certain that he would be one and, after I had known him for a short while, I was equally convinced that he would succeed in his aim.

Theodore, who was thirty-nine at the time, was something of a Renaissance man, a doctor, scientist, naturalist and a poet. He knew all about plants, flowers and trees, rocks and minerals, the lower forms of animal life, microbes and diseases, planets, comets and the stars; he was a student of the history and folklore of Corfu and enjoyed taking part in peasant dances; and he was devoted to poetry, writing his own poems in English and also translating from Greek to English the works of modern Greek poets. It was literature that drew Theodore to Larry.

But also there were the Indian and English connections which brought Theodore close to the entire Durrell family. Theodore's parents were cosmopolitan Greeks: his father worked in India for the international Greek merchant company of Ralli Brothers and married Caterina Ralli, the boss's daughter, who was born and educated in London. Theodore himself had been born in Bombay in 1896 and with his parents escaped the torrid summer months in the plains for the cooler climate and English society of the hill stations of India, including Kurseong and Darjeeling, where a dozen or so years later Lawrence Samuel Durrell would be the executive engineer of the Darjeeling Himalayan Railway and Larry would be at school. Theodore grew up speaking English as his first language and also, having been born in the Raj, he was a British citizen; he learnt Greek only at eleven, when his father retired to Corfu, where the Rallis had an estate.

Theodore Stephanides soon after he met the Durrells.

During the First World War Theodore served as a gunner with the Greek Army on the Macedonian front, and he served again in the disastrous Asia Minor campaign, which was fought to liberate the Greek-speaking population from Turkish domination but which ended with the destruction of Smyrna in 1922 and the expulsion of over a million Greeks from their ancient homeland.

In the same year as the fall of Smyrna, Theodore went to Paris to study medicine and specialised in radiology under Madame

Theodore in the Greek Army on the Macedonian front, 1917.

Curie. While there he developed his passion for astronomy under the tutelage of one of the leading French astronomers, Camille Flammarion, who wanted him to become his disciple and heir. Instead Theodore returned to Corfu, where he practised radiology, establishing the island's first X-ray unit in 1929; he was never well off, however, as he treated anyone who came to him whether they could pay or not. On the island he met and married Mary Alexander, who was of Greek and English parentage; her grandfather had been British Consul in Corfu and had retired to Bournemouth, where Mary was raised. Theodore and Mary had one daughter, Alexia, not much younger than Gerry and who became his closest childhood friend.

On top of these coincidences and connections, Theodore's interests and the richness and variety of his learning further bound him to each of the Durrells, as Gerry explained in *The Corfu Trilogy*.

> With Mother he could discuss plants, particularly herbs and recipes, while keeping her supplied with reading matter from his capacious library of detective novels. With Margo he could talk of diets, exercises and the various unguents supposed to have a miraculous effect on spots, pimples and acne. He could keep pace effortlessly with any idea that entered the mercurial mind of my brother Larry, from Freud to peasant belief in vampires; while Leslie he could enlighten on the history of firearms in Greece or the winter habits of the hare. As far as I was concerned, with a hungry, questing and ignorant mind, Theodore represented a fountain of knowledge on every subject from which I drank greedily.

* * *

'A month or two after I knew them,' recalled Theodore, that is in the late summer or early autumn of 1935, 'the Durrell family, including Lawrence and Nancy, all transferred

Margo, Nancy, Larry, Gerry, Mother at the Daffodil-Yellow Villa, 1936, and the villa, little changed, in 1996.

to the much larger Villa Anemoyanni.' This was Gerry's Daffodil-Yellow Villa near Kontokali, at Sotiriotissa, about five miles along the coast road north of Corfu Town. This contradicts Gerry's account, which makes it seem that the family remained at the Strawberry-Pink Villa for a year and a half, until the summer of 1936, and that they moved only to accommodate a sudden influx of Larry's friends. In fact the Strawberry-Pink Villa had been taken on a short six-month lease to see if the family liked Corfu, but it was always too small and once the lease expired at the end of the summer of 1935 it was time to move.

Standing on the side of a hill rising out of the sea, the Daffodil-Yellow Villa (though it was actually a faded pink) was an enormous and neglected Venetian mansion four storeys high, set amidst extensive grounds, overgrown and almost wild, with unkempt orange and lemon orchards and olive groves, and with melancholy cypresses and stout arbutus heavy with ripening berries.

Facing the sea was a stone-paved terrace shaded with a trellis of vines and evergreens, from where terraced gardens and a Venetian stairway descended to a wooden jetty projecting from the shore. A couple of small islands shimmered in the channel and in the distance loomed the hills of mainland Greece and Albania. To the left was Gouvia Bay, a smooth sheet of water used as a landing place for seaplanes, and beyond that the high hills shouldering Pantocrator, the highest mountain on the island.

It was Spiro who had found the villa and who organised the family's move from the Strawberry-Pink Villa with a minimum of fuss. Within three days of first seeing the Daffodil-Yellow Villa their belongings arrived, piled high on a procession of wooden carts which creaked and raised the dust all along the road from Perama to Kontokali.

The approach to the villa from the coastal road was through a stone gate and along a carriageway that wound through the orchards and olive groves, sweeping up to a broad flight of steps that ascended to a terrace and the entrance. Along the way the drive passed by the cottage of the villa's gardener and his wife, Lugaretzia.

'In a moment of misguided enthusiasm,' said Gerry, Mother engaged Lugaretzia to work for them in the villa. She was 'a thin, lugubrious individual' and sensitive; the slightest criticism of her work and she broke into tears, and so the family gave up criticising her at all. Her chief contribution to life at the villa was her hypochondria: the only thing that

The temperamental maid – Lugaretzia.

brought a glint to Lugaretzia's eye, a smile to her lips, was when the family would discuss her numerous ailments.

And so with everything in place the Durrells moved in.

* * *

Just beyond the villa was Gouvia, or Govino, once a Venetian port, though for many years its fortifications had been sinking deeper into the silt and the great naves of its arsenal, where shipwrights repaired the galleys of the Levant squadron, were roofless and gaping at the sky. However, the flying boats of Imperial Airways had recently brought new activity to the place, and the excitement of distant worlds. Gouvia Bay was a way station between England and Egypt and beyond; at Alexandria the route bifurcated, one heading south up the Nile to Khartoum and Lake Victoria, then on to South Africa, the other heading east to Baghdad, Karachi, Calcutta, Singapore and Australia.

When the Durrells wanted a new villa, Spiro knew where to look; he was familiar with Gouvia Bay, where the Short flying boats circled and hovered above its surface until their keels suddenly ripped open the polished emerald surface of the bay. 'Spiro is the favourite taxi-driver of the pilots', Larry wrote in *Prospero's Cell*; 'they like his Brooklyn drawl, his boasting, his coyness; he combines the air of a chief conspirator with a voice like a bass viol ... Prodigious drinker of beer, he resembles a cask with legs; coiner of oaths and roaring blasphemies, he adores little children, and never rides out in his battered Dodge without two at least sitting beside him listening to his stories'.

Spiro was moved when one young pilot asked to be driven to Canoni at four in the morning, just an hour before his departure. In the light of the car's headlamps they both clambered up the dew-drenched hillside overlooking Mouse Island, gathering narcissi and asphodel. 'It is the kind of little devotion that touches the raw heart of Spiro', reflected Larry, 'as he

Spiro with his taxi and local children.

pants and grunts up the slopes of Canoni, his big fists full of wet flowers, and his sleepy mind thinking of the English girl who to-morrow will touch this lovely evidence of the island's perpetual spring.'

* * *

These first months at the Daffodil-Yellow Villa, from the early autumn of 1935 through the spring of 1936, more closely match the account given in *My Family and Other Animals* than any other. For once in Corfu all the Durrells were under the same roof. There was plenty of space for everyone and the rooms were large. Larry and Nancy's room was bright and airy, with two large windows that were partly shaded by a great climbing vine which covered the side of the house. Very soon, noticed Theodore, the room became cluttered with books and dictionaries and files, which turned the room into a battleground between Larry and his mother. Mother would insist that he must keep his room tidy; Larry, who had just had his first novel *Pied Piper of Lovers* published in London and was close to completing his second, *Panic Spring*, insisted that he would not.

Apart from battling Larry over the state of his room, Louisa busied herself in her enormous stone-flagged kitchen improvising jams and lime chutneys while trying to ignore the drone of Lugaretzia's litany of illnesses and complaints. But meanwhile she was making little progress with her Greek, having trouble for example with the similarities between the words for flea (*psillos*), dog (*skilo*) and wood (*ksilo*), and was forever asking Lugaretzia to add more fleas or another dog to the fire.

But it could be hard to know if Mother was always as vague as she seemed to be, as, on that morning, recalled by Gerry, when she took Larry by surprise while he was complaining at breakfast about the quantities of insects in his honey, something that had long delighted Gerry and provided him with many new forms of insect life for his collection.

'Can't that fool Lugaretzia's husband collect honey in a civilised way?' Larry asked irritably. 'Must we have the entire insect population of Corfu embedded in it? French honey, after all, is as clear as amber.'

'Do you know what a French breakfast is?' asked Mother somewhat unexpectedly.

'What?' said Larry, unguardedly.

'A roll in bed with honey,' said Mother and gave a coy giggle.

Larry stared at her for a moment.

'Really, Mother', he said at last. 'I do feel that if you are going to tiptoe into the realms of sex you should be able to do better than that. I do hope you haven't gone about repeating that to all and sundry. They'll wonder how you ever came to conceive us all. Anyway, anyone trying to roll about in bed with this honey is liable to get a mortal wound in their genitals from a scorpion.'

'But Larry dear, it's a play on words,' Mother explained. 'I think it's rather clever.'

'Next time I go to Paris, I'll get you the works of Krafft-Ebing,' he said austerely, 'it'll help straighten out your sexual perspectives.'

'You always have to drag sex into everything,' said Margo. 'I think Mother's joke is very funny. I mean, imagine getting honey all over the sheets. It would be very comical.'

Larry groaned, picked up his book and his mail, left the terrace and went indoors.

'Well,' said Mother,. 'I would have thought he would have liked my being a little less narrow minded.'

'Who's this girl Honey,' asked Leslie interestedly. 'Is she from Corfu?'

At which Gerry left the familiar family tangle and returned to his animals.

As for the others, Leslie, Margo and Gerry each responded in their own way to their new home. Leslie immediately turned the verandah behind the house into a shooting gallery and to avoid shooting his family hung a large red flag outside whenever he was practising.

Margo began at the villa with three weeks in bed. Gerry says she had come down with a severe case of influenza after kissing the feet of the 1600-year-old mummified corpse of the island's miracle-working patron saint during a celebration at the church of St Spiridion in town.

'*Po-po-po*,' said Dr Androuchelli to Margo, with echoes of Dr Chakravati, 'remarkably unintelligent you have been, no? Kissing the saint's feet! *Po-po-po-po-po!* Nearly you might have caught some bugs unpleasant. If you kiss another saint's feet in the future I will not come and cure you. *Po-po-po!* What a thing to do!'

Margo in Corfiot peasant's costume.

In *My Family and Other Animals* Margo enthusiastically kisses Spiridion's feet hoping he will cure her acne; his healing powers were such that half the male children of Corfu were named after him. Margo herself never mentioned such an event, but she did admit to applying the holy water from Lourdes, given her by her governess in India, to a boil on her foot in Corfu – 'a consequence of going native, walking barefoot as the peasants did', but with no effect – an experience that diminished Margo's faith in holy water, 'but up till then I had been convinced!'

Gerry for the first time had his own bedroom. He also had a vast new garden to explore – and plenty of time to do so, as George Wilkinson had excused himself from coming up from Perama to tutor him. There were encounters with the new and strange in every direction: scorpions in the garden walls, tree frogs in the lemon and fig trees, lizards, snakes and tortoises on the hillside, and birds of all kinds, most notably swallows, which Gerry was able to observe at close hand under the eaves of the house where they built their nests.

There were also Gerry's weekly visits to Theodore in town. Theodore's initial invitation to tea and to look at his microscope slides had turned into a routine; Gerry was driven into town by Spiro every Thursday that autumn and winter, his pockets stuffed with matchboxes and test tubes of myriad creatures. 'It was an appointment that I would not have missed for anything.'

'Theodore's study was a room that met with my full approval,' said Gerry. 'Just what a room should be.' The walls were lined with bookshelves filled with volumes on freshwater biology, botany, astronomy, medicine, folklore and 'similar fascinating and sensible subjects'. Mixed in with these were collections of ghost and crime stories, so that Conan Doyle's *The Hound of the Baskervilles* was cheek by jowl with Darwin's *On the Origin of Species*, and Le Fanu's *Carmilla*, the story of a lesbian vampire, rubbed up against Fabre's *The Life of a Spider*, 'in what I considered to be a thoroughly well balanced library'. On one side of the room was a massive desk piled with X-ray plates, micro-photographs, scrapbooks, notebooks and diaries. On the other side was a microscope table with a powerful lamp and boxes full of Theodore's slides. The windowsills were lined with bottles and jars containing twitching and whirling freshwater fauna and a telescope stood gazing at the sky. Gerry and Theodore's talk went from fleas and spiders to tadpoles and vampires, from Greek mythology to the possibility of life on Mars – no

Margo, Gerry, Theodore, Mary, Mother and an unknown woman
at Villa Anemoyanni – the Daffodil-Yellow Villa.

matter what the subject, Theodore would open up some fresh
vein of fascinating discovery.

* * *

No hordes of Larry's friends descended on the Daffodil-Yellow
Villa, but the villa did have one visitor that winter of 1935–
1936, nineteen-year-old Alex Emmett, who had been at school

with Leslie and had known the entire family in Bournemouth. He arrived in time for Christmas. 'It is reputed that I nearly killed him', remembered Margo, 'by walking him right across Corfu without any water one day.' Margo was a great walker and it was with Margo that Gerry did much of his long-range exploring – dressed in a brightly coloured sweater so that Mother would be better able to pick him out at a distance. 'Gerry and I went everywhere together, into the fields with the workmen. We involved ourselves in every incident: births, marriages and deaths, and anything else that might come along.' Alex observed that Mother was still knocking back the gin, Leslie was cleaving to her and at the same time lost, while Gerry found refuge in his animals and his lessons with Theodore. Had it not been for Stephanides, Alex concluded, Gerry would have become lost too, like Leslie.

After a cool wet winter, the whole island vibrated with spring. 'It was apparent in the gleam of flower petals, the flash of bird wings and the sparkle in the dark, liquid eyes of the peasant girls.' And best of all, continued Gerry in *My Family and Other Animals*, 'In the water-filled ditches the frogs that looked newly enamelled snored rapturous chorus in the lush weeds.'

The time of water-filled ditches was the season Theodore had been waiting for.

> I think ... er ... you know ...' he would say, 'we might investigate those little ponds near ... er ... Kontokali. One of the reasons I particularly want to go ... er ... that way ... is because the path takes us past a very good ditch ... er ... you know ... that is to say, a ditch in which I have found a number of rewarding specimens.

Theodore would come and visit the Daffodil-Yellow Villa always immaculately dressed in suit and tie and stiff collar and wearing a Homburg hat, which contrasted with his nets and bags and boxes full of test tubes. He came every Thursday

Alexia botanising with Gerry.

for tea, arriving at the villa by carriage 'as soon after lunch as was decent', Gerry wrote in *My Family and Other Animals*. In fact he often arrived on foot, enjoying the walk from town, and Mary his wife and Alexia his daughter would follow in a carriage – though Gerry does not mention them at all in his book, nor even in his autobiographical fragments. Mary was 'a very beautiful lady', remembered Margo, 'very social and led a totally different life' to Theodore's. Leslie, who like all the other Durrells loved Theodore, thought that Mary was frivolous and did not appreciate him. But, in Gerry, Theodore found someone eager to learn, a serious boy without arrogance towards animals and the natural world in whom he might instil his values – and he began to look upon Gerry as a son, hoping that Gerry would someday marry Alexia. The hope seems to have been shared by the Durrell family; 'I remember hoping that Gerry would marry Alexia, although I didn't think he would – because of his great interest in animals. Which was his main interest, in animals. Women came later.'

On their expeditions Theodore and Gerry would prowl the ponds and ditches, Gerry seeking a terrapin, a frog, a toad or a snake to add to his growing menagerie, Theodore pursuing his interest in freshwater biology, carrying a little net to scoop up the smaller fauna, some almost invisible to the eye. And, as they marched from place to place across the fields and through the groves of olives, they sang this rousing nonsense song which gave new life to their tired feet.

> There was an old man who lived in Jerusalem
> Glory Halleluiah, Hi-ero-jerum.
> He wore a top hat and he looked very sprucelum
> Glory, Halleluiah, Hi-ero-jerum.
> Skimmer rinki doodle dum, skinermer rinki doodle dum
> Glory Halleluiah, Hi-ero-jerum.

Larry bought a guitar that spring and sang Elizabethan love songs, becoming more melancholy with the more wine he drank. His other favourites at this time were modern but hardly more upbeat, Jerome Kern's *Smoke Gets in Your Eyes* and *Miss Otis Regrets* by Cole Porter. Margo, who sang flat, also favoured the lovelorn and the morose, Gerry remembering her endlessly repeating *She Wore a Little Jacket of Blue*.

> She wore a little jacket of blue,
> She kept that little jacket of blue,
> And all the sailors knew
> Just why she wore his jacket of blue.

Theodore characteristically delighted in livelier tunes, *There is a Tavern in the Town* and *Waltzing Matilda*. And

Spiro would take to the road in his open-top Dodge singing his favourite, a song he picked up in America where it was number two in the charts in 1928, called *Oh I'm a Gay Cabellero*.

Oh I am a gay caballero
Going to Rio de Janeiro
With nice oily hair,
And full of hot air,
I'm an expert at shooting the bull-eo.
I'll find me a fair señorita
Not thin and yet not too much meat-a.
I'll woo her a while
In my Argentine style
And sweep her right off of her feet-a.

Mother did not sing but Nancy recalled the joy one rainy afternoon when Theodore visited with some records of Greek folk music and taught her and Mother the graceful, flirtatious and swaying movements of traditional Corfiot dances.

* * *

Gerry had long had a fascination with scorpions. The garden wall was home to great numbers of them and Gerry would observe them patiently, finding them weird but charming and not at all frightening; if you were careful with them, they would respect you. Gerry would capture scorpions and make them walk about in jam jars to see how their feet moved, and he would watch them dining on grasshoppers, moths and flies, but he could never figure out how they caught their prey – except when they ate one another. Going out to the wall at night with a torch, he would follow their mating rituals. If only he could keep a colony of scorpions in captivity he would be able to observe the entire cycle of courtship and reproduction. But the family had forbidden scorpions in the house ...

Meanwhile, since the start of Theodore's visits and their excursions together, Gerry had begun collecting creatures on an ever greater scale. His room was filling with specimens and Gerry was having to find space for new additions wherever he could around the house – with the occasional uproar if someone in the family found a beetle or frog where least expected.

All of which presented a problem to Gerry on the day he came upon a fat female scorpion in the garden wall who appeared to be wearing a fur coat. On closer inspection this

Gerry with a stuffed barn owl standing by a cage of his Corfu 'zoo'.

turned out to be a mass of babies clinging to their mother's back. 'I was enraptured by this family, and I made up my mind to smuggle them into the house and up to my bedroom so that I might keep them and watch them grow up.' He carefully put mother and young into a matchbox and rushed into the villa, but just then lunch was being served so he placed the matchbox on the mantelpiece in the drawing room and then joined the family in the dining room. What with dawdling over his food and sneaking bits of food to Roger, Gerry completely forgot about his scorpions. So it was with only the mildest interest that his gaze followed Larry, who had finished his meal and gone to the drawing room to fetch his cigarettes, bringing the matchbox back with him to the table and opening it.

Larry, who was 'talking glibly' and not looking at what he was doing, withdrew a match from the box. The mother scorpion, seizing her chance to escape, scuttled out with her babies on board. Feeling the movement of the scorpion's claws on the back of his hand, Larry glanced down to see what it was, and from that moment, as Gerry puts it, 'things got increasingly confused'.

Larry let out a roar of fright and with an instinctive flick of his hand sent the scorpion flying down the length of the table, scattering its babies everywhere, hiding under the plates and the cutlery. Lugaretzia dropped her plate, Roger leapt out from under the table wildly barking. Leslie and Margo screamed as the scorpion sped towards them and knocked it back and forth between them with their napkins until Margo attacked it with a glass of water which missed the scorpion but drenched Mother. Sensing now that the whole family was under attack, though he did not know by whom, Roger spun round and round the room barking hysterically and then went for the one outsider and bit Lugaretzia in the leg.

'It's that bloody boy again,' shouted Larry. 'Look at the table, knee-deep in scorpions, He'll kill the lot of us!'

A consequence of the scorpion panic was that Gerry was given an additional room, a large room on the first floor, in the hope that this would confine his animals to that part of the villa. The family called this room the Bug House; to Gerry it was his studio and here he kept his natural history books, his diary, microscope, dissecting instruments, nets, collecting bags and so on. The room housed his collections of beetles, butterflies, dragonflies and birds' eggs, as well as such curiosities as a four-legged chicken, which was a present from Lugaretzia's husband, the fossilised remains of a fish, a photograph of Gerry shaking hands with a chimpanzee and a stuffed bat.

Gerry had dissected and stuffed the bat himself ('it looked, I thought, extremely like a bat, especially if you stood at the other side of the room'), but he failed to cure it first. A disagreeable smell began to permeate the house for which Roger was initially blamed, but when finally the stench seeped into Larry's bedroom an investigation was launched and the source identified. Under pressure, Gerry was forced to get rid of the bat, but this early dissection and taxidermy work was to raise in his mind profound questions about the nature of life and his relationship to his own being and the magic of the whole – as he was to write sixty years later in one of his last autobiographical fragments:

I think it was because of these primitive dissections that I first started appreciating the complex and fantastic structure in which I dwelt – my body – and most of it functioning without any apparent direction from me, who was the owner or temporary inhabitant. I was unaware how my kidneys functioned. I gave them no orders and yet they continued to do their duty nevertheless. If I put out my hand to pick something up, I was aware that my brain had given my hand instructions to perform this task, and yet I was not even on speaking terms with my kidneys. Did a hedgehog, I wondered, give instructions to the web of muscles so that he rolled into a spiky ball when danger hove into view, or did it happen automatically? (I longed to dissect a cow or a horse, but I knew that the intricacies of smuggling so large a corpse into my bedroom would be discovered and put an end to.)

Then there was the amazing difference between various creatures. The difference between the musculature and bone structure of a bat and a bird, for example. After all, although they were bird and mammal, they both flew and so you would expect their internal organs to be the same. Then there was the difference between a lizard, a snake and a tortoise ... All this was fascinating enough, but when you got to the insects who, for the most part, wore their protective armour outside, the mind boggled at the shapes they had assumed and the incredible architecture and articulation of their body parts. Then of course there were the transformations as startling and bizarre as anything a stage magician could produce. The dragonfly larvae, like some strange steam shovel in the pond's depths who, when the time was right, would crawl up a leaf or twig and split open like a strange sandwich and from its uncouth interior would emerge the adult, hawk-eyed, wings glittering like a thousand church windows, and with a speed and manoeuvrability that no man-made flying machine could match ...

Leaf to bud, caterpillar to butterfly, tadpole to toad or frog, I was surrounded by miracles. I was surrounded by magic as though Merlin had passed through and casually touched the island with his wand.

* * *

One reason Theodore liked to visit the Daffodil-Yellow Villa on Thursday afternoons was to satisfy his passion for watching seaplanes put down in the waters of Gouvia Bay. Gerry describes in *My Family and Other Animals* how around teatime the Short Empire flying boat of Imperial Airways would arrive from Athens, having flown from India or Egypt and far beyond, en route to Southampton, which it would reach just over twenty-four hours later.

Theodore, in the middle of an anecdote or an explanation, would suddenly stop talking, his eyes would take on a fanatical gleam, his beard would bristle, and he would cock his head on one side.

'Is that ... er ... you know ... is that the sound of a plane?' he would inquire.

Everyone would stop talking and listen; slowly the sound would grow louder and louder. Theodore would carefully place his half-eaten scone on his plate.

Imperial Airways flying boat at Gouvia Bay.

'Ah ha!' he would say, wiping his fingers carefully. 'Yes, that certainly sounds like a plane ... er ... um ... yes.'

Mother would put Theodore out of his misery and ask if he would like to watch it land. This meant going up four flights of stairs to the attic, where the windows offered a clear view over the headland to the bay.

'Well ... er ... if you're sure ...' Theodore would mumble, vacating his seat with alacrity. "I ... er ... find the sight very attractive ... if you're sure you don't mind.'

The sound of the plane's engines were now directly overhead; the entire family abandoned the table and leapt up the stairs, following a joyfully barking Roger who raced on ahead.

The plane, like a cumbersome overweight goose, flew over the olive-groves, sinking lower and lower. Suddenly it would be over the water, racing its reflection over the blue surface. Slowly the plane dropped lower and lower. Theodore, eyes narrowed, beard bristling, watched it with bated breath. Lower and lower, and then suddenly it touched the surface briefly, left a widening petal of foam, flew on, and then settled on the surface and surged across the bay, leaving a spreading fan of white foam behind it. As it came slowly to rest, Theodore would rasp the side of his beard with his thumb, and ease himself back into the attic.

'Um ... yes,' he would say, dusting his hands, 'it is certainly a ... very ... er ... enjoyable sight.'

* * *

Communications were important for Larry, whose literary links were with London and Paris, a day away by air mail. Corfu and the other Ionian Islands had been under British rule for half of the nineteenth century and the impress of England was still felt. In the 1930s, said Larry, the island was far more developed than the rest of Greece, though 'it wasn't the Englishness that mattered, but the communications, the postal service, the degree of civilisation. Compared to Athens, Corfu was like Florence.' Larry was only partly living in Corfu; his thoughts and much of his sensibility were at the farthest end of the flying boat route, in England, in the suburban streets of Bournemouth and London, and in the Queens Hotel, which in the new book he was writing in Corfu he calls the Regina Hotel.

> Do not ask me why, at this time, on a remote Greek headland in a storm, I should choose, for my first real book, a theatre which is not Mediterranean. It is part of us here, in the four damp walls of a damp house, under an enormous wind, under the sabres of rain. From this nervous music rise those others, no less spectres, who are my mimes. I mean Tarquin, walking along the iced suburban streets ... I mean Lobo ... I mean Perez, Chamberlain, Gregory, Grace, Peters, Hilda ... When I am in the Regina I am dead again.

The book Larry was writing, his 'first real book', was called *The Black Book*, 'this chronicle of the English Death', finished on his twenty-fifth birthday at the house of Anastasius Athenaios at Kalami.

Chapter 6: **The White House at Kalami**

ON A BEAUTIFUL SPRING DAY IN 1936, Spiro drove Theodore and Larry and Nancy north from Kontokali along the coast road, a difficult journey during rainy weather and impossible when it was stormy. Here the ridges of Mount Pantocrator drove straight into the sea, creating a succession of coves but allowing little workable land, only the olive trees clinging to the slopes of the mountain in steep steps of terraces. Normally the journey was done by the daily caique which set out from Corfu Town for Kouloura across the narrow strait from Albania. In each direction the caique put in, when requested, at the little villages along this remote coast – exposed to the northern winter winds, parched in summer, a wilder Corfu, so different from the gentler, almost Italian lower half of the island. But today was fine, and as the big car bounced north along the broken road the afternoon sun struck obliquely through the olives, dappling the occasional colour-washed houses of ochre, of white, of mulberry, with light and shade.

Theodore had been invited to tea by Madame Gennatas and was asked to bring his new friends. The old widow lived in a fortified Venetian manor house at the port of Kouloura, the most beautiful of all the little coves along this coast, where a

Madame Gennatas' fortified Venetian manor house at the port of Kouloura.

horseshoe jetty sheltered red and blue fishing boats, and where waving pale green eucalyptus and dark jets of cypress rose above the sound of water faintly lapping at a pebble beach. The immensely thick walls of the manor house, originally pierced by loopholes, was now opened up by several French windows, which let out onto a wide stone terrace overlooking the sea. Here the visitors were served afternoon tea and listened to Madame Gennatas recall the Corfu she had known when she was a girl – and puzzled over her faint Liverpudlian accent, suggesting the possibility that her family had been cotton merchants who spent some time in Liverpool which was directly linked to the activities of the Greek cotton barons in Alexandria in Egypt, the two cities which then had the largest cotton exchanges in the world.

It was dark by the time Theodore, Larry and Nancy departed, but the bright moonlight helped Spiro navigate the

Dodge back to Kontakali. Along the way the talk was of the beauty of Kouloura and the dramatic landscape of the surrounding countryside. Nancy had long wanted to get away from the south of Corfu, away from the villas near town. 'I felt we'd been living too near the crowds – too tame. I was terribly keen on being in the wildest place I could find – most untamed.' Come morning, and Larry and Nancy decided to find some rooms in a peasant cottage up that way. Their thoughts were put into immediate effect by Spiro, who knew everyone: 'Don't you worries, Larry, I'll soon fixes it.' Ten days later, and against the wishes of his mother Louisa, who wanted him to remain at her villa in Kontokali, Larry was moving with Nancy into two rooms in a white-painted house overhanging the sea at Kalami, a sprinkling of four or five cottages round the headland to the south of Kouloura.

* * *

In moving out from the Daffodil-Yellow Villa Nancy misplaced what Larry called her 'beautiful anti-aircraft device', and without any means of contraception she soon became pregnant. Neither wanted a child just then; a chief purpose in coming to Kalami was to devote themselves without distraction to their writing and painting. But contraceptive devices were illegal in Greece and abortions too; only with some difficulty did they persuade a doctor in town, to whom they had been referred by Theodore, to declare that Nancy, so long and thin, 'was delicate and there was something slightly wrong with me', thereby justifying an abortion on health grounds.

'I held her head while she was coming round,' Larry wrote to a friend. 'God sicking froth and green stuff like camel shit from the ether. Then very quietly awake and laughing softly, as if at some incredible puckish and private joke. It's all very queer. All very untrue I feel. It's not fair. I don't feel we can ever make it up to women for what they are and for what they do for us.'

Nancy – 'I wanted just to absolutely drown myself in the sun and the sea.'

The crude reaction from some at the clinic outraged Larry. 'The Greeks are plain shits. Except for Spiro Halikiopoulos.'

Meanwhile the unfolding news of Italy's invasion of Ethiopia was full of foreboding and was brought closer to home when an Italian bomber, 'an aluminium giant fart', wrote Larry, made a reconnoitring flight over town. 'Of course we're scared shitless because if there's any place Benito wants more than Ethiopia it's Corfu. He smashed up the town with bombs in 1925, and had to be chased out by the British: and everyone is afraid he'll do it again. We're living in the extreme north of the island, and if there's trouble we'll have to get a fisherman to row us over to Epirus, and escape thence to Athens.' But, for the present, 'Sea dashes up under our drawing room windows, and the dolphins slink by all day as I sit and write this. I must go and bathe now. Naked, by God.'

The local Greeks, however, saw nothing godly about Larry and Nancy swimming in the nude. 'We used to go and bathe naked together,' Nancy remembered, 'keeping out of view of the fishermen because we didn't want to shock them too much – at that time peasants never even took their vests off in summer.' On one occasion, however, they had not noticed a church on a nearby promontory and the priest sitting on his porch with a full view of the beach. At the sight of their offence against God, tradition, morality and modesty, the priest rallied the youths of the nearby village, who took up positions in the hills above and pelted the bathers with stones. Larry and Nancy were forced to seek out isolated coves to avoid stonings, but they were seen nevertheless and their behaviour aroused indignation among many across the island.

For Nancy and Larry, however, their naked contact with the air and light and waters of Corfu was a sacred immersion. 'We were absolutely mad on taking off all our clothes,' recalled Nancy, 'I could never have enough. I wanted just to absolutely drown myself in the sun and the sea.'

One of their secluded bathing spots was a shingle beach shielded by a low cliff just north of Kouloura to which Larry, Theodore and Nancy would go by rowing boat, picnicking beneath the arms of an immense fig tree which overhung several gently inclined ledges of rock. Here they sunbathed and slipped naked into the blood-warm water of the rockpools, then plunged into the cold currents fed by streams spilling down from Mount Pantocrator. these 'stimulated his brain', Nancy said of Larry, who would bring a typewriter along and work on his latest book, the one that would become *The Black Book*. Then one day they found 'Angli' written in charcoal on one of the slabs of rock and knew that here too they were being watched.

A more secure bathing place was two coves south of Kalami where they found the shrine of a saint which was inaccessible except by water. Larry describes it in *Prospero's Cell*:

All morning we lie under the red brick shrine to Saint
Arsenius, dropping cherries into the pool – clear down
two fathoms to the sandy floor where they loom like
drops of blood. N has been going in for them like an
otter and bringing them up in her lips. The Shrine is
our private bathing pool; four puffs of cypress, deep
clean-cut diving ledges above two fathoms of blue
water, and a floor of clean pebbles. Once after a storm
an ikon of the good Saint Arsenius was found here
by a fisherman called Manoli, and he built the shrine

The shrine of St Arsenius near Kalami, photographed by Larry.

out of red plaster as a house for it. The little lamp is always full of sweet oil now, for Saint Arsenius guards our bathing.

Larry spoke of having two birthplaces: the one where you were physically born, the other the place where you wake up to reality. 'One day you wake up and it's there, and in your inner life, in your dreams; it's the place of predilection that comes forward and nourishes you.' That place for Larry was the shrine of Saint Arsenius, 'the place where we bathed naked all the time ... the place where I was reborn, where I finished *The Black Book*'.

* * *

Larry was inspired to write *The Black Book* after reading *Tropic of Cancer*, Henry Miller's ebullient and erotic depiction of underground Paris that had been published in 1934. In the summer of 1935, within a few months of arriving in Corfu and while still living near his family in Perama, Larry had been lent a copy of Miller's book by Barclay Hudson, an American painter sojourning on the island. 'Larry was absolutely bowled over by it,' recalled Nancy, while Larry declared to Alan Thomas, 'it's the greatest thing written in our lifetimes'. Where other books, 'all those tedious Ulysses and Chatterlies', got stuck in 'the morass and dirt of modern life, Miller comes out on the other side with a grin'. Published in Paris but banned for obscenity in Britain and America, Larry urged Alan to somehow get his hands on the book and, appealing to his instincts as a book dealer, told him, 'Even if you don't like it, the first edition value is going to be enormous.'

After reading the book, Larry wrote a letter to Miller in Paris that marked the beginning of a lifelong correspondence and friendship. 'It strikes me as being the only really man-size piece of work which this century can really boast of,' Larry wrote of

Tropic of Cancer. 'It really gets down on paper the blood and bowels of our time ... It finds the way out of the latrines at last. Funny that no one should have thought of slipping out via the pan during a flush, instead of crowding the door.'

To which Miller replied, 'Your letter is so vivid, so keen, that I am curious to know if you are not a writer yourself.'

By the end of 1935, his first year in Corfu, and once he had finished *Panic Spring* in December, Larry began writing *The Black Book*. He worked on it furiously for over a year with Nancy as his audience. The two were very close at this time: 'Nancy is as proud as punch, it being her book,' Larry wrote to Henry. 'I thought it was marvellous,' she recalled. 'I hadn't liked his first novel much – the *Pied Piper* was a bit dull – but *The Black Book* I thought was quite terrific.'

The Black Book was a radical departure for Larry from his first two novels. His first, *Pied Piper of Lovers*, completed in the summer of 1934 before any thought of going to Corfu and published by Cassell in the following year, has broad brush-strokes of autobiography. It tells the story of a boy, Walsh Clifton, born and raised in India, the son of a civil engineer. Sent to England for his education. Walsh briefly enters into London's bohemia but turns his back on it to live with the young woman he loves in a remote spot along the south coast of England overlooking the sea, not so far from Bourne-mouth. The girl has a heart problem; they know she will die at any time. Walsh and the girl decide to live by the moment, not as hedonists but happy to be alive, daily reborn into the here and now.

Panic Spring follows on, but loosely and at an angle. Larry began the book at Brindisi in March 1935 while travelling from England to Corfu and finished it at the Daffodil-Yellow Villa at the end of that year. The girl has died and Walsh, no longer the central character, is one of several expatriates, mostly British, who go to the Greek island of Mavrodaphne – which Larry based on Corfu – to heal from a wider malaise.

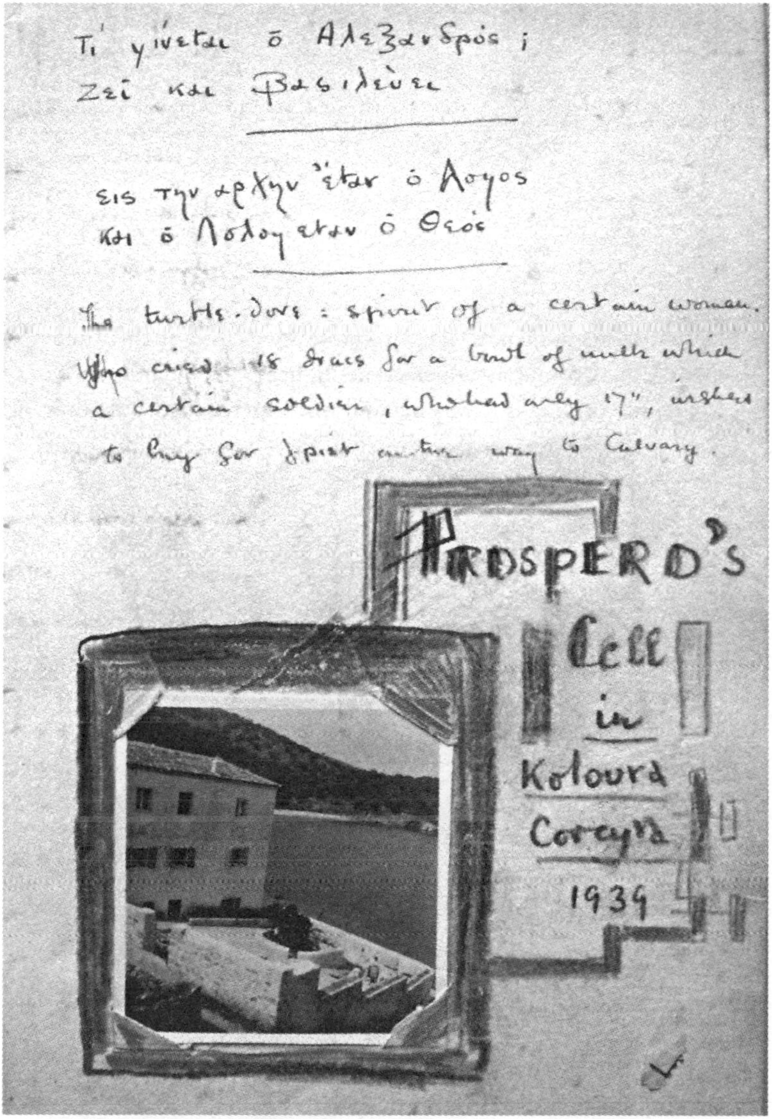

Τί γίνεται ὁ Ἀλέξανδρός;
Ζεῖ καὶ βασιλεύει

Εἰς τὴν ἀρχὴν ἦταν ὁ λόγος
καὶ ὁ λόγος ἦταν ὁ Θεός

The turtle-dove : spirit of a certain woman.
Who cried 18 dracs for a bowl of milk which
a certain soldier, who had only 17", wished
to buy for [?] on the way to Calvary.

PROSPERO'S
Cell
in
Koloura
Corcyra
1939

This page from one of Larry's journals shows the White House in 1939.
Kalami and Kouloura were used interchangeably. The Greek text above
begins with the familiar entreaty of sailors at sea in a storm: 'Alexander,
who lives and rules ...'

The White House at Kalami during Larry and Nancy's residence in 1937–38.

Pied Piper of Lovers had sold poorly and Larry was furious with the editors at Cassell, who had cut or altered passages they deemed offensive. So he was fortunate that Faber and Faber, where the poet T.S. Eliot was editor and director, saw merit in *Panic Spring*, which they published in 1936. To give it a fresh start they suggested that Larry use a pseudonym. He chose Charles Norden, after the character Van Norden in *Tropic of Cancer*.

'I am living at the Villa Borghese,' *Tropic of Cancer* begins. 'There is not a crumb of dirt anywhere, nor a chair misplaced. We are all alone here and we are dead.' Larry would do the same in *The Black Book*, where the epicentre of death is the Queens Hotel in Upper Norwood, or rather the Regina Hotel as he calls it in his novel, and like Miller finding this social and cultural death everywhere, throughout England, 'the English death', but also 'a European death as yet incomprehensible to most Europeans'. England and Europe were in their death throes, but the Mediterranean was still alive. 'The Mediterranean is the capital, the heart, the sex organ of Europe,' Larry said.

Larry finished *The Black Book* on 27 February 1937, his twenty-fifth birthday, added a dedication to Nancy, and sent his only copy of the typescript to Miller in Paris saying if he did not like it he could throw it into the Seine. Miller immediately replied in three long letters, the first dated 8 March beginning, '*The Black Book* came and I have opened it and I read goggle-eyed, with terror, admiration and amazement ... You are the master of the English language ... You have written things in this book which nobody has dared to write. It's brutal, obsessive, cruel, devastating, appalling. I'm bewildered still ... The whole thing is a poem, a colossal poem.'

But Miller added, 'Of course I don't expect to see Faber & Faber publishing it.' Larry had a three-book contract with Faber and Faber and so was obliged to offer them *The Black Book*. Miller was terrified that he possessed the only copy and before sending it on to London, he set to work with Anaïs Nin, his lover and patron, at making several copies more. When finally it went to Faber and Faber, T.S. Eliot replied to Larry on 28 June that he was 'very much impressed' but that it did contain certain words that presented difficulties. 'I shall be glad if anything can be done to make this book publishable in England; if not, I shall be glad to see it published abroad.'

Larry was tempted to expurgate his book so that it could be published by Faber, but Miller, who was a rock of artistic integrity, warned him against going down that route, and so it was published the following year in Paris by the Obelisk Press, which had done *Tropic of Cancer*, and carried Eliot's recommendation: '*The Black Book* is the first piece of work by a new English writer to give me any hope for the future of prose fiction.'

* * *

Living conditions at Kalami were primitive. Because the roads were washed out in winter and storms might interrupt the daily caique, Larry and Nancy subsisted on a diet of fish and often macaroni from a tin, though occasionally a lamb was killed. A sea cave or a well were relied upon to keep foods cool, while to boil water for a cup of tea could take twenty minutes of puffing on a charcoal stove. In winter the weather was often blowy and sometimes cold, and on an especially hot summer's day they would carry the whole table down to the water and dine with the Ionian up to their waists. And they had only a bedroom and a sitting room in addition to sharing the kitchen with the Athenaios family, who lived at the other end of the house.

So when Alan Thomas came from Bournemouth he was taken not to Kalami but to Sotiriotissa, what Gerry would call the Daffodil-Yellow Villa near Kontokali, and then to Paleo-castritsa on the far side of the island, where Larry and Nancy along with Theodore and his family all decided to rent rooms, turning Alan's arrival into a holiday of their own.

Alan disembarked at the quay in Corfu Town on 27 May 1937 and was met by Larry, Nancy and Pat Evans, a mutual friend of his and Larry's who had been taken on by the family as a tutor for Gerry. Alan was also introduced to Spiro, describing him in his diary as 'a great Rabelaisian character, nominally a car driver, but also one of the outstanding characters and general rogues on the island'. Arriving at Sotiriotissa, Alan wrote in his diary that 'Mrs Durrell is away and Leslie is in charge, another reunion. Leslie, whom I remember as a shy adolescent boy, has developed wonderfully under the sun. Both physically and in character.'

The Durrells on Corfu in 1938: Leslie, Spiro, Larry (with the gun), Gerry's tutor (and Margo's 'Homeric lover') Pat Evans, Mother and Nancy.

After lunch at Louisa's villa, which Alan noted was 'pale pink' (Daffodil-Yellow was Gerry's invention), Leslie joined them for the drive to Paleocastritsa, where after a swim and tea Leslie returned to the villa, while Pat, who had waited in Corfu long enough to see Alan, set off on a month-long walking tour through Epirus to Macedonia. It was a diversion from what Larry called his 'Homeric love' for Margo.

In *My Family and Other Animals* Gerry has Pat appear as Peter, 'a tall, handsome young man, fresh from Oxford, with decided ideas on education which I found rather trying to begin with. But gradually the atmosphere of the island worked its way insidiously under his skin, and he relaxed and became quite human.' Gerry persuaded Pat that instead of receiving English lessons he should write his great novel of the flora and fauna of the world, 'four fat notebooks in which was written my great Epic of going round the world collecting animals, taking my entire family with me', a page-turner with each chapter ending on a thrilling cliffhanger, making the reader eager to know more, 'Mother being attacked by a jaguar, or Larry struggling in the coils of an enormous python.' The epic was packed in a trunk to be forwarded when the family left Corfu, but in the rush and confusion it was lost. 'It would, I feel,' wrote Gerry in his memoirs written near the end of his life, 'have made interesting reading now'.

But things did not go well with Pat, Gerry continues in *My Family and Other Animals*. 'Mother had discovered, as she so delicately put it, Margo and Peter were becoming "too fond of one another"'. Pat's services were dispensed with and Margo took it badly, locking herself in her room and howling. 'Yes, I did have a crush on Pat Evans', Margo said years later. 'It was inevitable that we would get together, we did things together, you know. We rode horses and we went through the olive groves. And he introduced me to opera, *La Traviata*. He used to come to us in Bournemouth. And I liked him then; well, who wouldn't? He was great.'

Amid the upset of having her relationship with Pat broken off, Margo began grossly over-eating and was putting on a pound a day. 'Margaret was in a very bad way,' recalled Nancy. 'She began to get very fat, I mean she really did get awfully fat.' But the cause turned out not to be a broken heart, rather a glandular condition for which Louisa took Margo to London, and took Gerry too, leaving the Daffodil-Yellow Villa in Leslie's hands. 'Coming from the calm, slow, sunlit days of Corfu, our arrival in London late in the evening was a shattering experience,' Gerry writes in *The Corfu Trilogy*. 'So many people were at the station that we did not know, all hurrying to and fro, grey faced and worried.'

Back in Corfu, at Paleocastritsa, Alan Thomas spent his first day swimming in the warm Ionian and walking with Larry and Nancy up to the Byzantine monastery built on a crag overlooking the sea, 'an amazing situation, like living in the sky'. At nightfall they dined outdoors under thatching at their rented cottage and talked themselves to sleep. 'This is a glorious place,' wrote Alan in his diary. 'I despair of giving any idea of it.'

On another day they sailed south in the *Van Norden*, Larry's sailing boat, which 'rode the sea like a bird', and landed at Mirtiotissa, a sand beach under a great cliff where they stripped and dashed into the sea – 'the water was like warm

Larry at Paleocastritsa.

milk'. Alan had not bathed naked since schooldays: 'It is an exhilarating feeling to have the water caress the whole of your body as you slide through it.'

They were all living in the same stone cottage at Paleocastritsa. An American painter called Maurice Koster was living in one half but offered two of his four rooms to Larry and Nancy. Theodore, with his wife Mary and his daughter Alexia, lived in the other half of the cottage. Alan talked a good deal with Theodore, his deliberate and accurate way with English coupled with his wide knowledge and a dry sense of humour making him a delightful conversationalist and the possessor of bizarre stories.

'Mainly we discussed death, how to avoid and come by it', Alan noted one afternoon. The most effective way to commit suicide, said Theodore, was holding a revolver in the mouth at a forty-five degree angle, but not a .22 calibre.

'I would advise either of you, should you contemplate suicide,' Theodore said to Alan and Larry, 'to use a .38 or preferably a .48.'

'Surely', said Larry, 'if you used a .48 you would blow your head off.'

'But that would be your object, wouldn't it?' Theodore replied, and then went on to discuss the various symptoms of syphilis until 'between us', thought Alan, 'we seemed to have them all'. And 'he also told us how to get out of a whirlpool'.

In between times they listened to Theodore's collection of Greek folk songs, talked about peasant dances, turned over the latest news from the civil war in Spain, and discussed the effect of a major conflagration on the price of vegetables. 'I have become a worshipper of the sun, and beneath it nothing matters. I live in a vortex of light', Alan wrote in his diary. 'Time is of no account here. I haven't wound my watch for a week. Larry frequently writes dates 1938.'

After ten days they returned to Corfu Town, Nancy, Larry, Theodore, Alan, Spiro, and also Leslie, who had fetched up at

Nancy and Theo on the caique to town.

Paleocastritsa after spending the night on a fishing expedition with his Greek friends. The road rose steeply and twisted back and forth upon itself, some of the hair-pin bends so sharp that Spiro had to reverse the car once or twice to get round, while all along the way he blasted his horn and shouted to everyone he passed.

'He is a character, that man,' Alan wrote in his diary.

Sitting at the wheel in his shirt sleeves, white chauffeur's cap on one side of his head, brown eyes almost hidden in little bags of wrinkled flesh, cigarette in mouth, upper lip scarred. With everyone he is on familiar terms, to him they are Nancy or Alan. Or else 'dear'. Always excepting Larry whom he addresses as Lord Byron.

Twisting down the narrow cork-screw road with its loose surface and undefended drops, swinging round hair-pin bends with inches to spare.

Leslie: It's a dangerous drive this, Spiro.

Spiro: Not with me, dear.

The idyll of those days, the idyll that Alan experienced, was not shared by Nancy, who later said, 'I never liked Alan Thomas. In fact I disliked him.' She did not remember a great deal about his visit to Corfu, 'except that he annoyed me as usual, and particularly in that I thought he was living in a dream-land and not in reality at all. He wanted the whole Corfu thing to be a sort of Dream in the Luxembourg – romantic and wonderful. And it was a time when I remember Larry and I were quarrelling very violently.' On one occasion they were quarrelling at breakfast while Alan was there. Later in the day she saw his diary open and he had written something like '"sitting having breakfast in this magical place with the wonderful sunshine streaming in and the delightful conversation with the Durrells", etc, etc. And I remember my feeling of intense irritation. He was completely ignoring reality so far as I was concerned.'

Alexia, who was in Paleocastritsa with her mother throughout the summer while Theodore would go back and forth to his radiology work in town, remembers Larry and Nancy, who also spent much time in Paleocastritsa after Alan left. Alexia recalled them living in complete harmony. Larry had taken up painting and they worked busily throughout the day with never a cross word between them. But Alexia remembered that, while Larry never minded the little girl watching him, Nancy, who would set up her easel in some quiet spot, would shoo her away.

Larry and Nancy had come to Corfu to each freely enjoy their artistic pursuits. Each was fiercely independent and

Larry and Nancy at Kalami on the *Van Norden*.

demanding of their art. But the attention attracted by Larry's writing was beginning to open up their hermetic world and to alter the balance between them. In Nancy's response to Alan's diary remarks, one has the sense that she felt she was being intruded upon and put to one side.

In mid-July, Louisa, Margo and Gerry returned from London. Then on 10 August, five and a half months after completing *The Black Book*, Larry and Nancy took the ferry to Brindisi and from there the train to Paris to meet Henry Miller and Anaïs Nin. They would stay in Paris and in London for eight months altogether before returning to Corfu in April 1938. And in November that year they would go to Paris and London again, not coming back to Corfu until May 1939, seven months later. While Gerry in *My Family and Other Animals* teasingly depicts Larry as a would-be writer living at home with the rest of the brood, struggling against scorpions to write deathless prose, the reality was that Larry had entered the innermost literary circles in England, where he became such a familiar sight that Dylan Thomas, after bumping into Larry yet again in a London pub, asked him, 'Has somebody moved Corfu?' In truth, from August 1937 to the outbreak of war in September 1939, Larry and Nancy spent more time in France and England than they did in Corfu.

In September, a month after Larry and Nancy's departure, Louisa and the family moved out of the Daffodil-Yellow Villa to what Gerry would call the Snow-White Villa, not far from the Strawberry-Pink Villa at Perama. According to Gerry the idea was Larry's, of course.

> 'Well, if we're going to be invaded by relations, there's only one thing to do', said Larry resignedly.
>
> 'What's that?' inquired Mother, looking over he spectacles expectantly.
>
> 'We must move, of course.'

That is what Gerry says in *My Family and Other Animals*. Yet no relations were expected. And Larry was not there. But as Margo, speaking of her brothers, once said, 'I do not trust writers.'

Chapter 7: **The Snow-White Villa**

BEFORE LARRY AND NANCY SET OUT for Paris, in August 1937, they arranged with Anastasius Athenaios, the owner of the house in Kalami, to add another storey; the Durrells would pay for it and live on the upper floor, while Anastasius would have his house enlarged at no cost to himself. Work was already underway by the time they left; Anastasius, or Totsa as he was known, was a man of many abilities, a fisherman, a carpenter, and he had built the original stone house himself. Now with the help of a few local men, and working by rule of thumb, he set to work.

Larry set one condition. As Theodore recounted the story, Larry repeatedly told Totsa, 'I want two *big* windows that will take up almost the whole of the wall facing the sea. I *insist* on two big windows. I *must* have *two* big windows so that I can look out on the sea and feel as if I were actually riding the waves.' Totsa gently and patiently explained that delightful as two big windows would be in summer, they would offer no protection against the icy winds blowing in from the snow-clad mountains of Albania in winter. The occupants would freeze and storms could whip the sea as high as the upper storey and smash through such big windows, drenching everything

The White House and Kalami photographed in 1955. Larry and Nancy
paid for the addition of the upper storey which was built during the
winter of 1937/38.

within. But Larry brushed these excuses aside. 'From here to
here. See, I'm marking it so that there should be no mistake.
Two *big* wide windows.' And away went Larry and Nancy to
France and England for eight months.

The White House, as it became known, was being transformed into the handsome dwelling overlooking the bay at
Kalami that we see today. And for Larry and Nancy the spacious upper storey of several rooms was to be their year-round
home. Whatever the disturbances in the outside world, they
meant to be in Corfu to stay. This is probably one reason why
Louisa decided to move; Larry and Nancy would no longer be
under her roof even occasionally and the Daffodil-Yellow Villa
was now too large.

The family's new house was smaller but grand, and also closer to town, at Cressida, very near the Strawberry-Pink Villa at Perama where the Durrells had made good friends with the Condos family who had a fish taverna down the hill. In *My Family and Other Animals* Gerry called it the Snow-White Villa.

> Perched on a hill-top among olive-trees, the new villa, white as snow, had a broad verandah running along one side, which was hung with a thick pelmet of grapevine. In front of the house was a pocket-handkerchief sized garden, neatly walled, which was a solid tangle of wild flowers. The whole garden was overshadowed by a large magnolia tree, the glossy dark leaves of which cast a deep shadow. The rutted driveway wound away from the house, down the hillside through olive-groves, vineyards and orchards, before reaching the road. We had liked the villa the moment Spiro had shown it to us. It stood, decrepit, but immensely elegant, among drunken olives.

Built in 1824 in the Georgian style and owned then and still now by the Palatiano family, the villa was once a weekend retreat for the British High Commisioners, until 1864, when Britain transferred Corfu and the other Ionian islands to Greek rule. The villa stands on a prominent rise overlooking the shallow Halikiopoulou Lagoon, with a far view towards Canoni, while on the flat lands on the near shore were what Gerry called the Chessboard Fields, an intricate pattern of saltpans created by the Venetians to collect brine but now flooded by fresh water from the hills so that each small patch of earth, framed with canals, was richly cultivated and green with vegetables, figs and grapes.

This was one of Gerry's favourite hunting grounds, for the landscape of ditches and tiny islands and the lush undergrowth harboured a multitude of creatures, among them the ancient and wily terrapin called Old Plop that eluded capture by Gerry for a month or more. But it was easy to get lost here; in the pursuit of a plopping amphibian or a fluttering butterfly you might cross the wrong little wooden bridge between islands and lose your bearings in the labyrinth of reeds and fig leaves and stalks of maize. For Gerry, though, he was never far from a welcome.

Most of the fields belonged to friends of mine, peasant families who lived up in the hills, and so when I was walking there I was always sure of being able to rest and gossip over a bunch of grapes with some acquaintance,

Villa Number Three, or as Gerry called it, the Snow-White Villa, at Cressida.

or to receive interesting items of news, such as the fact that there was a lark's nest under the melon-plants on Georgio's land.

In this way Gerry became what he called in his unpublished autobiographical fragments a 'human newspaper', an itinerant gatherer and broadcaster of local news.

> In Corfu, within a six mile radius, I was the medieval equivalent of the town crier or a sort of human newspaper. Some of the peasant communities would perhaps only see each other once or twice a year at a fiesta. So I, travelling around as I did, brought the latest news, whether Agatha had died or whether Spiro (no – not that Spiro but Spiro with the blind donkey – Oh! that one) – well, his potato crop had failed. *Po! Po! Po!* they would cry in horror, *and he had the whole winter stretching before him, potatoless.* St Spiridion preserve him.

* * *

One day when Gerry had gone to the Chessboard Fields and was plunging for water snakes in the shallows of the lagoon he became aware of a young man who had arrived silently and was now squatting nearby and watching him with wry interest. He was 'a short, stocky individual whose brown face was topped by a thatch of close-cropped fair hair, the colour of tobacco. He had large, very blue eyes that had a pleasant humorous twinkle in them, and crows' feet in the fine skin at the corners.' Gerry supposed him to be a fisherman from some village farther along the coast.

'Your health,' the man greeted Gerry with a smile.

Gerry returned the greeting while trying to wrestle the snake he had just caught into his basket without letting the first one escape. The snakes were quite harmless, Gerry knew, but he fully expected the man to lecture him on the deadliness of water snakes; to Gerry's surprise, however, he remained silent, watching intently as Gerry wrestled the writhing snake into the basket. Gerry then produced the grapes he had helped himself to from the fields, offered half to the man, and they sat together silently.

'You are a stranger?' the man asked after a while. Gerry said he was English and that he lived with his family in a villa up in the hills. But instead of interrogating Gerry further, as peasants usually did, wanting to know all about each member of the family, their ages, gender, work and so on, the man again surprised Gerry by seeming to be entirely content with his answer.

Then Gerry said he would go down to the sea to wash the caked silt off his body and look for some cockles to eat. 'I will walk with you,' the man said. 'I have a basketful of cockles in my boat; you may have some of those if you like.'

As they walked through the fields towards the sands, the man pointed to his rowing boat in the distance, pulled up on the shore. Gerry asked if he was a fisherman and where he was from.

'I come from here, from the hills', he replied. 'At least, my home is here, but I am now at Vido.'

The reply puzzled Gerry, for Vido was the local prison island lying off the town of Corfu, and as far as he knew entirely uninhabited except for convicts and warders. Gerry pointed this out to him.

'That's right,' he agreed, stooping to pat Roger as he ambled past, 'that's right. I'm a convict.'

I thought he was joking, and glanced at him sharply, but his expression was quite serious. I said I presumed he had just been let out.

'No, no, worse luck,' he smiled. 'I have another two years to do. But I'm a good prisoner, you see.

Kosti the convict (front) with a local fisherman.

Trustworthy and make no trouble. Any like me, those they feel they can trust, are allowed to make boats and sail home for the weekend, if it's not too far. I've got to be back there first thing Monday morning.'

Once the thing was explained, of course, it was simple. It never even occurred to me that the procedure was unusual. I knew one wasn't allowed home for weekends from an English prison, but this was Corfu, and in Corfu anything could happen.

Gerry's curiosity to know what his crime had been was interrupted as they reached the boat and he saw, tethered to the stern, an immense black-backed gull. Gerry at once stretched out his hand to stroke its back.

'Be careful, watch out; he is a bully, that one!' said the man urgently.

But his warning came too late. Gerry was already gently running his fingers through the bird's feathers. The gull crouched, his beak opened slightly, his eyes narrowed – and he did nothing.

'Spiridion!' said the man in amazement. 'He must like you; he's never let anyone else touch him without biting.'

Gerry asked the man where he had got such a magnificent bird. Crossing over to Albania in the spring, he said, to catch some hares. The gull was small then, but now, he said, addressing the gull, it had become a 'fat duck, ugly duck, biting duck, aren't you, eh?' The gull opened one eye and gave a short sharp yarp of agreement.

He had tried to get rid of him, said the man. He could not catch enough fish to feed him, he went about biting everyone, and the prisoners and wardens did not like him, but each time he let him go he came back. One weekend soon he would take him across to Albania and abandon him there.

'But if you want him you can have him,' the man said.

Gerry could hardly believe his ears. He would have given his soul for such a wonderful bird and now incredibly it was being offered to him almost carelessly. How the family would greet the arrival of a bird the size of a goose and with a beak like a razor never entered Gerry's mind; without hesitating he took up the bird to carry it home under his arm.

'He knows his name', the man remarked. 'I call him Alecko. He'll come when you call.' At which Alecko waggled his legs and, squinting up at Gerry, yarped again. 'You'll be wanting some fish for him. I'm going out in the boat tomorrow, about eight. If you like to come we can catch a good lot for him.'

As the man was pushing his boat out into the waters of the lagoon, Gerry took his chance and as casually as he could asked him his name and why he was in prison.

'My name's Kosti,' he said smilingly over his shoulder. 'Kosti Panopoulos. I killed my wife.'

'Your health,' he called as his boat went out. 'Until tomorrow.'

* * *

'What on earth's that?' gasped Mother.

'What an enormous bird!" exclaimed Margo. 'What is it, an eagle?'

'Where did you get him, anyway?' asked Leslie.

Gerry explained about his meeting with Kosti, but said nothing of the water snakes; all snakes terrified Leslie. And without thinking, Gerry added that Kosti was a convict.

'A convict?' quavered Mother. 'What d'you mean, a convict?'

I explained about Kosti being allowed home for the week-ends, because he was a trusted member of the Vido community. I added that he and I were going fishing the next morning.

'I don't know whether it's very wise, dear,' Mother said doubtfully. 'I don't like the idea of your going about with a convict. You never know what he's done.'

Indignantly, I said I knew perfectly well what he'd done. He killed his wife.

'A murderer? said Mother, aghast. 'But what's he doing wandering round the countryside? Why didn't they hang him?'

'They don't have the death penalty here for anything except bandits,' explained Leslie; 'you get three years for murder and five years if you're caught dynamiting fish.'

'Ridiculous!' said Mother indignantly. 'I've never heard of anything so scandalous ... Anyway, I won't have you wandering around with a murderer,' said Mother to me. 'He might cut your throat or something.'

And so the next morning Gerry went fishing with Kosti and, when they returned with enough fish to keep Alecko fed for a couple of days, Gerry asked his friend to come up to the villa and meet Mother.

Nervously Mother sat on the verandah, the few words of Greek she knew having flown her mind in the face of the ordeal of having to make small talk with a murderer, while Kosti in his faded shirt and tattered trousers drank a glass of beer and Gerry translated.

'He seems such a nice man', Mother said after Kosti had taken his leave; 'he doesn't look a bit like a murderer. I thought he'd look, well, you know, a little more murderous.'

* * *

Early in 1938, just a few months after Louisa moved into the Snow-White Villa, Theodore's expertise as a freshwater biologist led him to join an anti-malarial campaign funded by the Rockefeller Foundation. Greece had been cursed by malaria since classical times and the disease continued to be responsible for over a million cases and five thousand deaths a year; this out of a population of less than seven million. Throughout this year and the next, his work would be in Cyprus and also in the north of Greece at Thessaloniki, and he would return to Corfu on only occasional visits.

Theodore had been a mainstay of the Durrell family and his absence would be deeply felt; and for Gerry it was the loss of the one person, apart from Larry, whose learning and authority he valued and accepted. 'If I had the power of magic', Gerry once remarked, 'I would confer two great gifts on every child – the enchanted childhood I had on the island of Corfu, and to be guided and befriended by Theodore Stephanides.' Gerry was losing Theodore and soon he would lose Corfu.

The family itself was changing; the Durrell children were hardly children any more, and Larry, who turned twenty-six in 1938, had always known Corfu as an adult. Now Leslie became twenty, Margo eighteen, and Gerry celebrated his thirteenth birthday. Gerry illustrated an invitation to his party with a prancing and rather Rabelaisian-looking depiction of

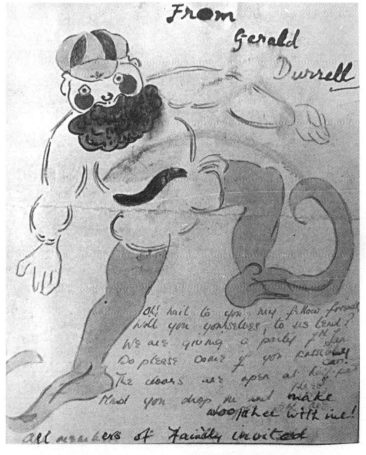

Gerry's invitation to 'make whoophee' on his thirteenth birthday.

himself inviting his guests to 'make whoophee with me', but he had passed beyond childhood into the more uncertain feelings of puberty.

In an autobiographical fragment Gerry recalled a woman nuzzling up to Theodore's legs and saying,

'You know, I have an open fire – I throw salt in it when it's blazing'.

'Indeed', said Theodore, 'why, er, do you do that?'

'Because it makes a blue flame, blue as a man's eyes, blue as yours.'

'Ah!' said Theodore, 'It is interesting that the reason the salt makes the flame blue is ...'

She watched him adoringly and pressed on, asking him about Adam and Eve.

'I have tried myself – in private you understand – to sew fig leaves so that they cover the – the – parts which on the human body they – reputedly – covered and I found them to be recalcitrant in a modist's sort of way.'

* * *

On 15 April 1938, eight months after they had left for Paris and London, Larry and Nancy returned to Corfu. Theodore was briefly back on the island then and accompanied Spiro, who collected them at the port and drove them to Kalami. Spiro parked the car on the road above and they descended the winding mountain path from where the house came into distant view, with its extra storey whitewashed and roofed with tiles. But when they finally reached the beach and could see the house from the seaward side, Larry burst into a roar of rage. Facing out over Kalami Bay the upper floor had two small windows.

'I have rarely seen Lawrence more indignant and upset,' Theodore recalled. 'At first he wanted to turn right around and return to the car and leave Kalami for ever. It was with great difficult that Nancy and I persuaded him to change his mind. But for many weeks, even after the upper floor had been made into a beautiful and comfortable home, he would scarcely speak to Athenaios.'

But they made it up when the autumn storms proved that Totsa had been right all along. 'It was extremely problematical if the upper floor could have been lived in,' said Theodore, 'if the two *big* windows had been actually installed.'

With plenty of space now at the White House in Kalami, Margo and Gerry would come and stay. Margo thought Larry was 'a very pompous creature in a way', while Nancy was 'a very gentle, a lovely person; she was often painting and reading – she was a quiet person'. But Margo thought Larry and Nancy got on well enough. 'I don't actually see it as a tempestuous marriage. I didn't look at it that way.'

Larry continued to concern himself with Gerry's education, having already introduced him to Rabelais during the early days at the Strawberry-Pink Villa, and since then giving him books to read such as *The Story of My Heart* by the utopian English nature writer Richard Jeffreys and *Social Life in the Insect World* by Jean-Henri Fabre, who was an influence on Darwin; and exposing Gerry to Beethoven which Larry played on his gramophone: 'He was surprised to hear me whistling a bit of Beethoven's Eighth,' Gerry remarked in one of his autobiographical fragments.

* * *

'One of the nice things about Larry was that he was absolutely determined that Gerald was going to do life his own way. He didn't want him messed up. He didn't want him sent to schools that were going to take him the wrong way. When you went to see them, they did have a bath, but Gerald always had creatures in the bath.'

Spiro with ballerinas Veronica and Dorothy.

This is Veronica Tester speaking. Like her Australian friend Dorothy Stevenson, she was a ballet dancer and they came to Corfu in the summer of 1938 after meeting Larry in London the winter before: 'He was full of life and energy. Dabbling in everything, lots of interests outside just poetry. I had always wanted to go to Greece, and I remember him saying, well, we've found our place in Corfu, we're going to be building it, and you must come and stay.'

In those days Kalami was so small, just a handful of houses, that one often spoke of it as being Kouloura, which was the nearby port for the daily caique back and forth to Corfu Town. Veronica arrived first; Dorothy came later.

'They were in their house at Kouloura. So I stayed there with Nancy. I hadn't met Nancy before, but we got on very well, and I stayed there the whole summer.' Then Margo came to stay for about ten days. 'She was a nice girl. One didn't know if she was coming or going, but she was a very nice girl. One of the things we did together was we walked up Pantocrator; and we walked up there, and it was very very hot, really hot. There's a road now, but there wasn't then, only donkey tracks.'

They all got up very early in the morning, at about six, and would sit on the big flat rock alongside the house where they would breakfast and look across to Albania. 'Beautiful and quiet and lovely.'

'And then Larry, he used to work all the morning; he worked very hard. Nancy used to paint all the morning. I used to go off exploring; I learnt enough Greek to be polite and go up to villages, and they all pinched my back, they had never seen a bare one, wearing shorts and a shirt. I had a lovely time doing that, looking at flowers and stuff.'

As time passed Veronica became increasingly aware of the contrast between the north and south of the island. 'All the people in the north wore their black clothes and blue and white, and they carried things on their backs; and then as you go down to the south of the island which had the Venetian history and where Larry's mother and Margo and Gerald and Leslie were, you go down there and you had these women carrying things on their heads and wearing coloured things; the top was biblical and the bottom was Venetian, a complete divide. And then you had Corfu Town in the middle with people playing cricket and the Brits turning up. It was a magical place. And Larry was extremely aware and very sensitive to all these different things, so it was fun being with him and enjoying these different aspects of it.'

After Dorothy arrived, Larry decided they should all go off on an expedition, so he and Veronica sailed round the top of Corfu to Paleocastritsa while Spiro took Nancy and Dorothy by road. 'It was a most beautiful empty beach, and there was a very large rock in the middle of it which gave it shade in the middle of the day. We stayed there two or three weeks, I should think. The goatherd used to come down from one side in the morning, and the shepherd came down the other way in the morning on the beach, but nobody else was there. I think there are little bits in *Prospero's Cell* that refer to us,' said Veronica.

Prospero's Cell is Larry's lyrical evocation of Corfu written in Alexandria after the island and the world were struck by war. As Veronica said, 'Before the war was another world.' It is written in the form of a series of impressions entered into a journal. So for 9 August 1938 Larry writes:

> Riding south from Paleocastrizza in a fair wind we come to Ermones beach just before dawn; and swimming ashore in the grey half light we build in gleaming sand the figure of a gigantic recumbent Aphrodite. N and Veronica model the face while Dorothy and I shape the vast thighs. We give her a crown of pebbles for pearls and a belt made from withes of sapling, like snakes. She lies staring at the lightening sky, her mouth open in an agonizing shriek, being born. While the sea creeps up and gnaws her long rigid fingers.

Veronica and Larry sunbathing near Kalami.

By first sunlight we are away again, wondering what
the wide-eyed fisher-boys will make of this great relief
in sand. Aphrodite rising from the foam.

'Larry was twenty-six; he was very beautiful and had all
this lovely blond hair. He was very brown; he was very ath-
letic, loved swimming. We all used to swim with no clothes all
the time. Nancy was a lovely long thin blonde creature. Such
a contrast to Larry in build. The fact that we were a couple of
strange females around was by the way; in those days people
did not go to bed like they do now.'

Throughout their lives, Veronica said, she and Dorothy held
memories of this magical time. 'We really did feel all the Greek
gods and goddesses and nymphs and dryads – you see, Larry
produced that atmosphere. He was terribly good at this sort
of thing. You could feel Cupid and Psyche. It was absolutely
wonderful.'

Nancy also remembered that time. 'I don't think Larry was in love with either of them at all. He wanted to have a flock of young girls. They were twenty, I suppose, and it was wonderful for him to dance with two dancers, pretending to be Pan, while they danced naked on the beach.'

'When I left him' – Nancy left Larry during the war – 'when he was trying to persuade me not to leave him, he said, "I've only been unfaithful to you twice. Once was behind a rock with Dorothy Stevenson. And once with ..." I've forgotten her name, in Paris. And I think it was probably true that he wasn't much more unfaithful than that.'

* * *

From time to time, says Gerry in *My Family and Other Animals*, the Durrells would decide to throw a big party, and this time, as it was already September, they decided to call it a Christmas party, to which they invited everyone they could think of, not forgetting people they disliked. Preparations began far in advance, almost guaranteeing, as Gerry observed, that nothing would go according to plan. On the day itself Mother was in her kitchen preparing vast quantities of food, her eyeglasses misted over, oblivious as always to the approaching storm. On this occasion the predictable mayhem was owed to the animals, in particular to the creatures Gerry had brought back from the Chessboard Fields, Old Plop and Alecko and the water snakes.

The detonator came when Gerry, for innocent and intricate and outlandish reasons, filled the bath with water snakes and Leslie, who abhorred nothing more than a snake, leapt into the tub without looking, just as the first guests were arriving. All talk was abruptly frozen by a bellow from inside the house, then Leslie appeared on the verandah clad in nothing but a small towel.

'Gerry,' he roared, his face a deep red with rage. 'Where's that boy?'

'Now, now, dear,' said Mother soothingly, 'whatever's the matter?'

'Snakes,' snarled Leslie, making a wild gesture with his hands to indicate extreme length, and then hastily clutching at his slipping towel, 'snakes, that's what's the matter. That bloody boy's filled the sodding bath full of bleeding snakes,' said Leslie, making things quite clear.

'Never mind, dear, it's really my fault. I told him to put them there,' Mother apologized, and then added, feeling that the guests needed some explanation, 'they were suffering from sunstroke, poor things.'

This led to a general eruption, with Larry protesting with fantastical exaggerations, Margo bitterly accusing Larry of interferring, Leslie telling everyone to shut up, Margo insisting she has as much right as anyone to air her views, Mother haplessly telling her children not to quarrel, not to shout – and then, when the dogs in the street outside began to howl, attracted to Dodo, one of the Durrells' dogs, who was on heat, the entire family would turn round and bellow, 'Shut up,' causing the more nervous of the guests to spill their drinks.

* * *

A ten-year-old girl called Vivian Iris Raymond was at this Durrell party, or one very much like it, and has left her own impressions. She was born in Cephalonia, one of the neighbouring Ionian islands, and belonged to a British merchant family who had been resident there since the early nineteenth century and evidently regarded themselves as some sort of aristocracy. She spelt her name in the masculine form with an 'a' (instead of Vivien) because she had been named after an admiral of the Royal Navy.

We once visited Mrs Durrell and the rest of the family in their home near Corfu Town. We were served a meal outside. Gerald, Lawrence's youngest brother, was a few years older than me. He seemed to be a very big boy. He ignored me ... The Durrells all talked at once, shouting across the table and calling from the kitchen door, behaviour I associated with my Greek cousins but not with English people. At one point a ruckus broke out when someone emptied a kitchen bowl of water into the garden. It had contained Gerald's tad-poles. Many years later in his book, *My Family and Other Animals*, Gerald described this scene in fabu-lously exaggerated terms; the tadpoles had become snakes, flung far and wide amid shrieks of horror. As an adult I enjoyed the book for its entertaining sto-ries, but was offended by the mocking tone towards the Greeks. The Greeks are exuberant, excitable people, full of energy and abundant self confidence. But they are not clowns. Indeed, it had seemed to me that the Durrells had been the clowns.

Theodore Stephanides was a friend of Vivian's family and would sometimes visit them in Cephalonia. 'He was a most upright man, in the literal and figurative sense, and sported a trim ginger beard .... He was a man of a great many parts.' His wife Maria was 'a very tall thin English lady' whose guests would sit in a very large drawing room drinking tea. 'Mrs Stephanides would serve steaming English scones with cream and strawberry jam from Harrods. Theodore would stay in his study where he had his microscopes, biology spec-imens in various tanks and a library that covered one entire wall. His study opened on to the drawing room. Men who were visiting would often take their scones and join Theodore in his study.'

Vivian's family knew Madame Gennatas. Theodore told them she had a strange accent in Engligh but they never noticed

Corfu 1938 Dorothy Veronica Kerkera Larry

At the White House, summer 1938: Anastasias 'Totsa' Athenaios (Larry and Nancy's landlord and grandfather of Tassos, the present owner) is second left; Veronica and Dorothy are next to him, centre; and Larry is far right.

because they always spoke to her in Greek. They would visit her by yacht, as did the King of Greece, who always called at Kouloura in summer.

That was how Vivian Iris Raymond's family came upon Nancy and Larry, who lived just round the Kouloura peninsula in the bay of Kalami.

> We visited them quite a few times ... The established British community was not comfortable with the Durrells' bohemian lifestyle. The Durrells were not members of the professional or officer classes, and were certainly not gentry. They were quite unlike any other British people on the islands at that time. They associated with the peasants and villagers in a way that offended both those below and above their station. This is not because the establishment looked down on

the villagers. We were genuinely fond of our servants ... The villagers had a uniquely Greek sense of pride and bearing that permitted no acknowledgement of inferiority. However, they knew their place. There were many subtle rules that defined just what interactions were appropriate across the social strata. The Durrells did not understand these conventions. They did not fit.

According to Vivian, the Durrells' behaviour caused offence throughout Corfu. They were known to have been stoned by the village priest and boys for bathing naked and, 'worse still,

The nineteen-year-old Margo, in a thoroughly unrevealing dress.

they took visiting friends on their skinny dipping excursions, including unaccompanied young ladies from England. That was noticed'. Margo also attracted attention by sunbathing in the olive groves 'in her scanty sun frock with matching frilly knickers. This was offensive to the villagers in those parts. Word spread.'

Larry and Nancy certainly had no business calling themselves artists:

> At the Durrells' I saw a painting by Nancy. It represented Adam and Eve standing in a bathtub. The bathtub was deep but transparent so Adam and Eve were visible in their nakedness, sporting exaggerated pubic hairs that had been painted in hard angry strokes. Their bodies were grotesquely ill-proportioned ... I was shocked by the ugliness of Nancy's painting. Lawrence talked loudly and drank too much. He slapped the local peasant fisherman on the shoulders, and invited him to eat with the family, and served him whisky. It seemed to me that the Durrells were ill-disciplined, with pretensions but without the sensitivity or upbringing to participate in the ancient and settled culture of Corfu. I had heard Mummy's friends talk about degenerates, a term I had not understood, but decided that they must have been referring to people like the Durrells.

* * *

Following the deparure of Dorothy and Veronica, and a month after the Munich Agreement in September 1938 gave Hitler a slice of Czechoslovakia, Nancy told Larry that she wanted a child. 'A little red general with fat legs, to ride into Czechoslovakia on a white horse? What sort of animal vegetable mineral is a woman's mind?' Larry wrote to Henry Miller. The matter was put off a year, and early in November Larry and Nancy again travelled to Paris and London.

Gerry seeing his tutor – possibly Kralefsky, the bird fancier – in Corfu Town.

Early in 1939 Margo decided it was time that she returned to England. She had always been in two minds about whether it had been right to leave Malvern Girls' School. 'Corfu was an escape, in a way,' she recalled. 'I was doing very well at Malvern. I could have had a career, you see, which I sometimes wish I had done.' Now she returned to England and entered art school.

Following close behind was Maria Condos. The Durrells were very close to the Condos family in Perama, especially Leslie, who served in the local police force run by the Condos father, and also Margo, for whom they were a second home. Maria Condos had been the Durrell family maid and now she was going to England, possibly sponsored by Louisa's always practical and helpful cousin 'Aunt' Prue who was buying up rental properties in London and would have found good use for Maria, at least until the family arrived; Maria's immigration documents were stamped on 15 March. A month later Mary Stephanides and Alexia also left Corfu for England.

Larry had been away for months with no definite date of return, and Theodore was only occasionally on the island, leaving Gerry, who had recently turned fourteen, without any effective supervision. At the conclusion of *My Family and Other Animals* Mother is returning with the family to England on the advice of Gerry's tutor, the fantasist and bird collector Mr Kralefsky, who was urging a proper education for Gerry.

But in fact the Durrells were being driven from Corfu by the growing threat of war. On 7 April the Italians invaded Albania; in less than a week their victory was complete. The Italian Army supported by the Navy now stood barely more than two miles across the strait from Corfu. Then Grindlay's Bank, Louisa's financial advisors in London, warned that in the event of war she might be cut off from funds if she remained abroad.

In June 1939, Mother and Leslie and Gerry closed the door on the Snow-White Villa and left Corfu.

Chapter 8: **The War and the Scattering**

Larry had been trying to get Henry Miller to visit Corfu for years. Now, on the eve of war, Henry decided to take a holiday. Hitler had grabbed the rest of Czechoslovakia in March and Mussolini had occupied Albania in April; in July 1939, Henry sailed from Marseilles for Greece.

It was almost high noon, as Henry tells it in *The Colossus of Maroussi*, his account of his travels in Greece, when his boat pulled in at Corfu where Larry was waiting on the dock with Spiro Americanos. After an hour's drive they were at Kalami and before sitting down for lunch they went for a swim off the big black rock in the front of the house. 'I hadn't been in the water for nearly twenty years.' Nancy and Larry, who were 'like a couple of dolphins', took Henry to the shrine of Saint Arsenius where 'we baptised ourselves in the raw.' Nancy enjoyed Henry's visit and remarked how agreeable Larry was compared to how 'pesky' he had been during the visit of the ballerinas the summer before. But Nancy was less than happy with the English girl that Henry brought along, 'this strange girl Meg Hurd that he psychoanalysed', and when later Henry made love to Meg at the shrine of Arsenius, Larry crossly took it as a violation of his sacred place.

Henry Miller and Larry 'baptising themselves in the raw'.

Larry's letters to Paris had been marvellous, Henry recalled, but their descriptions of Corfu seemed a bit unreal. 'They caused a certain amount of confusion in me, owing to the fact that the dream and the reality, the historical and the mythological, were so artfully blended. Later I was to discover for myself that this confusion is real.'

Once a week Henry, Larry and Nancy would go into town on the caique and visit Spiro at his home in Canoni with its view over Pontikonisi, Mouse Island. 'In the evening', Henry says, 'Spiro sits here dreaming of his life in Rhode Island when the boot-legging traffic was in full swing.'

Theodore was staying briefly at Kalami when Henry came to Corfu. Theodore found him to be an amusing companion, a great talker and man of extreme energy who never seemed able to keep still – traits that reminded him very much of Larry despite their completely dissimilar physical appearances. Theodore also noted that Henry was a remarkable success with the locals. 'Without knowing a word of Greek, he seemed to be able to understand them and make them understand *him*. Also he was very fond of clowning and had very humorous and mobile features with which he could send his audience into roars of laughter.' Theodore himself was struck by Henry's lively curiosity in every subject, as when they would sit out in the evenings on the sun-heated rock by the White House and look up at a sky filled with stars and Henry would ask Theodore countless questions about astronomy; or when Henry, who, like Larry, took a great delight in Corfu wildflowers, 'especially the lovely pink cyclamen which had just begun to appear before he left the island', would collect wildflowers of every kind and bring them to Theodore, asking him for their names. 'It came as a great surprise to him when he discovered that there were a good many specimens that I could not name.'

As for Henry, he thought Theodore was quite simply 'the most learned man I have ever met, and a saint to boot'.

'At Kalami', said Henry, 'the days rolled on like a song.' Sometimes he wrote a letter or painted a watercolour, but he had no interest in picking up a book. In the evenings he talked and sang with Nancy and Larry or he stood on the rocks on the edge of the water and with a telescope he surveyed the stars.

In August Larry called on Madame Gennatas. Probably Nancy and perhaps Henry came along too. He gave her a copy of *Panic Spring* and inscribed it, 'To Madame Gennatas on her travels with the good wishes of her neighbour and friend. Charles Norden alias Larry. Kouloura 1939. August.' Madame Gennatas was going away.

* * *

Out of the blue one day in August, Margo appeared. Her months away in England had sharply reawakened the love she felt for Corfu and its people, for the island she called paradise. 'I decided Corfu was compelling and I came straight back.' Margo moved in with her friends the Condos family, who lived in Perama, at the foot of the hill below the Strawberry-Pink villa – father and mother and Costas and Katerina (and there had been Maria too before she went to work for the Durrells in England).

Margo shared in the great sense of excitement everywhere at the approach of war. In the early morning of 1 September Germany invaded Poland; Britain and France declared war on Germany two days later. Greece was neutral and Italy was still neutral, but there was the widespread feeling that a general European conflagration was about to begin.

'War was declared while I was at Perama', Margo recalled. 'I got a little note from Spiro, and it said, "Don't tell a soul! War has been declared!"'

'That was when the men disappeared; the very night when war was declared. It was a very emotional scene, everywhere, because everybody had lost their men, they'd all been sent to various camps. And Spiro Americanos immediately came to the rescue and took me and all the girls to find their men in all the army camps all over Corfu.'

Perama had no electricity and so no radio, and Margo and her friends would walk every night across the pedestrian causeway at the mouth of the lagoon to Canoni, where Spiro lived with his wife and children, to hear the most up-to-date war news.

Every able-bodied Greek on the island was mobilised, boats unloaded flour and bullets, a detachment of Cretan infantry landed in the north, joining four regiments standing at the defences opposite Albania. The men of Kalami and Kouloura, Larry's landlord Totsa Athenaios among them, were sent inland to a secret arms dump. Only the women were left and the uncomprehending children weeping in the garden.

'Leslie and I always swore to defend Corfu against the Italians', Larry afterwards wrote to his poet friend Anne Ridler in London, 'and we fought the whole thing out during the winter shoots, taking into account everything, including fleet movements. Ill luck found him in England.' Corfu Town was swarming with people trying to escape. 'Such passionate farewells, so many tears, so much language, it made one deaf. I had nothing to say goodbye to except the island, and it seemed already lost.'

At the White House in Kalami Larry and Nancy destroyed papers, books and paintings, emptying cupboards and packing clothes. A dazzling green rain fell on the glassy surface of the bay, while darkening clouds and viscous black water filled the strait towards Albania. 'Standing on our balcony overlooking the sea it seemed like the end of the world.'

But Margo was going nowhere. 'I wanted to stay and sit it out with my Greek family. I was definitely prepared to go into the fields and help them. I thought Lawrence was a bit oafish for dashing off. I did say goodbye to them at the port of Corfu.'

Goodbye to Larry and Nancy and Henry, who joined the general rush to get away, but you will find no mention of Margo remaining on the island in Gerry's *My Family and Other Animals*, no mention of Margo at all in Larry's *Prospero's Cell* nor in Henry's *The Colossus of Maroussi*. As Margo said, 'I never know what's fact and what's fiction in my family.'

* * *

Larry, Nancy and Henry went to Athens carrying introductions from Theodore to his literary friends, among them George Seferis, the future Nobel Prize-winning poet, and George Katsimbalis, publisher and editor of *Nea Grammata*, the leading literary magazine in Greece, and a spellbinding raconteur. Their encounter was the beginning of Henry's great journey round Greece with Katsimbalis and the best

Henry and Theodore and Nancy on the Acropolis 1939.

book Henry Miller ever wrote, *The Colossus of Maroussi* (Katsimbalis, an outsized man in every way, lived in the Athens suburb of Maroussi).

But Henry's journey with Katsimbalis was not immediate. Larry and Theodore found temporary posts with the British Embassy in Athens, working for its Information Services, translating Greek newspaper articles into English and writing and printing an official bulletin to counter the propaganda emanating from the German Embassy. Henry meanwhile was cross with himself for having needlessly, as he saw it, interrupted his island holiday, and after about ten days in Athens felt a longing to return to Corfu. Though war had been declared against Germany, the Italians announced their intention to remain neutral, so Henry 'saw no reason why I should not return and make the most of the remaining days of summer.'

Henry went to stay at the White House in Kalami, where Spiro sent his son Lillis to give him some Greek lessons. When

Larry in Athens with George Katsimbalis, the Colossus of Maroussi, 1939.

Lillis finally went back to town, Henry was left alone. 'A wonderful period of solitude set in ... It was the first time in my life that I was truly alone.'

Not quite alone, according to Margo. 'Lawrence asked me to look after him, and he said, "Don't let anybody swindle him", which I thought was a typical Lawrence remark at that point. I did look after Henry, and I found him very charming. He did use a lot of bad language, but then, you know, I was used to that language. He just was very genial. He came swimming, and was absolutely like a grandfather. Lawrence said I was safe because I was one of the family.'

As autumn came to Corfu the rains set in. In those days only a goat path connected Kalami with the road above, the road into Corfu Town, and day by day the path was becoming muddier and more difficult to climb, and even the road itself would become occasionally impassable when severe storms touched off landslides of rocks and trees.

Henry was thinking it was time to leave Kalami before he was marooned there for the winter when Nancy showed up to collect some household belongings; she was returning to Athens on the same boat that afternoon, and on a sudden impulse Henry joined her. That was the last time either of them ever saw Corfu.

* * *

Margo remained in Corfu, going into town at night from Perama, mixing with people, among them the crews of the Imperial Airways flying boats. They were flying up from Africa, stopping in Corfu, then continuing over Italy and eventually to their home base in England – which from 1 September had been transferred from Southampton to the greater safety of Poole harbour, within view of Bournemouth. On one of these nights in town she met Jack Breeze, an Imperial Airways flying boat chief engineer.

Margo at a crossroads in southern Africa with her husband Jack Breeze,
flying boat chief flight engineer, whom she met in Corfu.

'And he said that it was absolutely ridiculous thinking that
you could hide yourself as a peasant and work in the fields and
you won't be found out. And he said, if you're going to marry
me you have to go back to your mother immediately. And actually in the end I did flee, although I didn't really want to go.'

Just after Christmas 1939, Margo boarded one of the last
Imperial Airways flying boats out of Corfu and by the New
Year she was home in Bournemouth with Mother and Leslie
and Gerry.

* * *

On 28 December 1939, Henry Miller sailed from Piraeus, the
port of Athens, for New York, where he immediately began
writing *The Colossus of Maroussi*. There he had a letter from
Lillis, Spiro's son, from which he learnt that during his last days
in Greece, as he was saying goodbye to friends and waiting to

board his ship for America, 'Spiro was getting ready to die' in his vine-wreathed house on Nausicaa (Nafsika) Street in Canoni.

'My poor father died with your name in his mouth which closed forever. The last day, he had lost his logic and pronounced a lot of words in English as: "New York! New York! where can I find Mr Miller's house?" He died as poor as he always was. He did not realise his dream to be rich.'

* * *

Nancy gave birth to a daughter, Penelope, on 4 June 1940 in Athens. After attempting to get a posting in naval intelligence, Larry accepted a job from the British Council in Kalamata, deep in the Peloponnese. His purpose there, apart from teaching, was to show a British presence in a port town which relied heavily on agricultural exports to Germany and was a target for German propaganda, not least from the German School whose director was secretly an army officer.

That autumn on 28 October the Italians, who had already declared war on Britain in June, gave Greece an ultimatum to hand over its principal defences or face invasion. The Greek prime minister General Ioannis Metaxas famously said '*Oxi*' ('No!') and when the Italians launched their attack the outgunned and outnumbered Greeks resisted fiercely and drove the Italians scuttling back into Albania. But as everyone realised the Greek victory could only be a prelude to a brutally effective German intervention.

It came in April 1941. Leaving Corfu to the Italians, the Germans overran the whole of Greece within weeks. From Kalamata there was no escape except by sea. Fleeing in an overloaded caique, sailing by night to avoid German dive bombers, hiding in island coves by day, Nancy and Larry and their infant daughter survived the perilous three-day voyage and arrived in Crete, from where they were taken by a military vessel to safety in Egypt.

Larry with Penelope at Kalamata, from where they escaped the German
occupation of mainland Greece by taking a boat to Crete.

As Larry recalls in these last lines of *Prospero's Cell*, which he wrote in Alexandria, the images he held in his mind during their escape from Kalamata, memories of their lost world, were of Corfu:

> In April of 1941, as I lay on the pitch-dark deck of a caique nosing past Matapan towards Crete, I found myself thinking back to that green rain upon a white balcony, in the shadow of Albania; thinking of it with a regret so luxurious and so deep that it did not stir the emotions at all. Seen through the transforming lens of memory the past seemed so enchanted that even thought would be unworthy of it. We never speak of it, having escaped: the house in ruins, the little black cutter smashed. I think only that the shrine with the three black cypresses and the tiny rock-pool where we bathed must still be left.

* * *

When Mother returned to England with Leslie and Gerry, she rented a flat off Kensington High Street in London. The Germans had not yet begun their bombing offensive and the family settled into a routine of sorts. They saw Aunt Prue and various friends, among them Veronica Tester, who remembered their flat as 'uncomfortable', and her brother the actor Desmond Tester. Gerry found London fascinating, and dressed for the first time in trousers, not in shorts, he set about exploring the city.

In an autobiographical fragment Gerry recalled seeing Charles Laughton in *The Private Lives of Henry VIII*, a tell-all biography which runs through each of the King's five marriages. 'Entrance – Bed room – even now remember things I do for England and pan down to tiny feet,' Gerry wrote. This scene that had attracted Gerry's attention followed Henry's short-lived happiness with Jane Seymour, who dies in childbirth.

Reluctantly the King is now about to consummate his political marriage to the German princess Anne of Cleves. He stands outside her bedchamber and sighs, 'The things I've done for England,' while the camera pans down to his stockinged feet. 'Saw *Henry* 5 or 6 times and each time learned something new from it,' Gerry wrote.

As well as frequently going to the cinema, Gerry regularly visited the nearby Museum of Natural History or would go off to the zoo. Soon he got a job as a junior assistant in a well-stocked pet shop where he demonstrated such a caring knowledge of the fish, the tortoises, the snakes, the lizards and the rest that he was quickly promoted. But it was pale fare to what he had known in Corfu, and in another of his unpublished autobiographical fragments he contrasts in an impressionistic way his inner life with the lives of English boys his age:

> The bright caiques like dishevelled kingfishers, flashing in the bay below nuzzled by the tiny Mediterranean tide. Every day was Christmas – unlucky him, disgruntled urchin jealous from the English waterlogged muffin on which he lived. One can only assume that his childhood – if he had one – was trailing behind him like some sort of English ectoplasm – whereas I was trailing behind me something he could not understand – a childhood like a magic carpet.

For Mother, London was only temporary; she was drawn to Bournemouth, the one place she had ever felt settled in England, and by the end of the year had bought a house at 52 St Albans Avenue. It was here that Margo arrived when she returned from Corfu at the very end of 1939 and where, early in the new year, Leslie gave her away in marriage to Jack Breeze. Jack had been flying the Africa run via Corfu from Poole harbour, a few miles away, which by then had become the only point where civilians could arrive by air in Britain or depart, with special non-stop trains running between London and Bournemouth

Leslie with a firm grip on Mother at Bournemouth during the War. Gerry, now a head taller than the others in the family, is on the right.

West station. In April 1940 Britain's passenger air services were reorganised; Imperial Airways was merged with British Airways which had operated solely within Europe, and the two became British Overseas Airways Corporation (BOAC). Now the airline posted Jack to South Africa and he took his young bride Margo with him.

From South Africa over the coming years Jack and Margo moved northwards, first to Mozambique, then to Ethiopia, from which the British were dislodging the Italians who had occupied it in 1935. By some mischance she fell into Italian hands and gave birth by Caesarean section, without

Margo in Mozambique, on the Zambezi river.

anaesthetic, to their first son, named after her brother Gerry, in an Italian-run prisoner-of-war camp. Finally, towards the end of the war, Jack and Margo were posted to Egypt and lived in Cairo, but though Larry was working only a three-hour train journey away in Alexandria, they never met up.

Also in Egypt during the war was Pat Evans (Gerry's tutor 'Peter' in *My Family and Other Animals*), whose 'homeric love' for Margo, as Larry described it, had evolved into a 'huge emotional mess'. Though the son of devout Quakers, Pat served in the Royal Tank Regiment during its desert contests with Rommel in Egypt. Then in 1943 he joined the Special Operations Executive (SOE), a secret organisation set up to conduct espionage and sabotage in occupied Europe. Pat served in northern Greece in 1943–44, working with the Greek resistance against the Germans, and ending the war with the rank of major.

* * *

Theodore Stephanides joined the British Army in Greece and as a medical doctor with the rank of lieutenant in the Royal Army Medical Corps stayed with the British forces throughout the battle of Crete until the island's fall at the end of May 1941, when he was among the last to be evacuated to Egypt. Posted to a military hospital in Cairo, Theodore soon tracked his friend down at the 'Lunatic Park', as Larry called the Luna Park Hotel, 'a rather ramshackle place that the authorities had requisitioned to house British refugees, a terrible place and terrifically overcrowded', though at least Larry and his family had a room to themselves.

Theodore and Larry had last seen one another on a November day in Athens in 1939 after their temporary work as translators at the British Embassy came to an end. There was much to talk about: remembered friends and recent adventures, not least the hair-raising escapes each had made from the Greek mainland to Crete, Stephanides in an antiquated Greek merchantman that was dive-bombed three times en route, Larry and his family dodging the Luftwaffe in an overloaded and listing caique. 'But their luck held', said Theodore, and after arriving safely at Alexandria they were taken to Cairo, where Larry soon found employment in the British Embassy publicity section.

The following summer the German Army, under the command of General Rommel, advanced across the desert out of Libya and stood within striking distance of Cairo. Early in July 1942, in the panic that followed called 'the Flap', Nancy and Penelope, along with other British women and children, were evacuated to Palestine. A month or so later Larry had a letter from Nancy in Jerusalem saying she was not coming back. Their marriage was over.

That autumn, as the guns of the Battle of Alamein were shaking the ground beneath people's feet, Larry was posted to Alexandria as British Information Officer. His task was to keep his eyes open and to ensure that the local newspapers, published in English, French, Greek, Armenian and Arabic, were fed with leads for appropriately upbeat stories, which often meant writing the copy himself. 'Lawrence was now in his element,' observed Theodore, who was soon transferred to a military hospital at Amriya immediately west of Alexandria; in a city whose atmosphere owed so much to its numerous Greek population, 'he was now his own boss and he was able to make good use of his knowledge of Greek'. Here Larry began filling notebooks with material that would eventually find its way into his *Alexandria Quartet*, and here he met a dark and sultry Alexandrian girl, Eve Cohen, who would become the model for his mysterious character Justine.

Theodore visited Larry several times in Alexandria, once for two weeks in December 1943: 'where I spent one of the nicest Christmases I had ever enjoyed. By this time Lawrence knew all about Alexandria, and he showed me the sites of some of its ancient monuments, including that of the Library and the famous Pharos. It was very interesting to look at the places where these famous monuments had once been, but, alas!, no ruins even of them still existed.'

* * *

Theodore might have said almost the same thing about Corfu. Just a few months earlier, on the night of 13 September 1943 and all through the following day, the Germans bombed Corfu and destroyed large parts of the town. The Italians, who had occupied the island, had surrendered to the Allies on 3

Theodore (left) in a makeshift medical centre in North Africa.

September after British and American troops landed in Sicily and on the mainland at Salerno; now the Germans were taking over Corfu to stop it passing into British hands.

German incendiary bombs destroyed churches and municipal buildings, Venetian houses and whole neighbourhoods, especially targeting the Jewish quarter. They bombed the Pension Suisse where the Durrells had first stayed, and they killed many people, including Gerry's tutor Mr Kralefsky (whose real name was Krajewsky) and his mother, as well as his birds, and they killed the father and mother of Theodore Stephanides. Corfu Town burnt for three days; the rubble from the devastation was used to build the runway of Corfu's airport, built on land reclaimed from the Halikiopoulou Lagoon.

Theodore did not return to Corfu again for twenty-four years, until 1967, when he helped Gerry make the BBC's *Corfu, Garden of the Gods*.

* * *

Towards the end of 1942, as Gerry was approaching eighteen, he received his call-up papers; from his appearance he seemed an entirely fit and healthy young man. Margo and Leslie took after their mother, who was small, and Larry, who stood no more than five feet two inches, took after Louisa too. Gerry was the one member of his family who took after his father in height; he now stood nearly six feet tall. But his old problem from the days before he went to Corfu had returned; he was continuously plugged up with catarrh – or, as the military medical examiner put it, according to Gerry, 'Your sinuses look like the Black Hole of Calcutta.'

Instead of being taken into the Army, he was offered a choice: to work in an armaments factory or on the land. Taking to his bicycle, Gerry looked for a suitable farm, not one that grew crops but one with animals, and soon, just north of Bournemouth, he found a farm with a few cows and twenty-two horses. Gerry spent the rest of the war mucking out the cows and grooming the horses and giving lessons to young ladies wanting to learn to ride. And all the while fixing on his childhood plan, to have a zoo of his own.

With the end of the war in Europe in May 1945, Gerry wrote to the Zoological Society of London, whose zoo housed the largest number of animals in the world. He was invited to an interview. At length he told the superintendent of London Zoo about his own zoo in Corfu, about collecting animals and displaying his intimate knowledge of animal habits, to which he was listened with the greatest patience and respect. And

Leslie's photo of Maria Condos, on the back of which he wrote 'Jolly nice'.

afterwards received a letter saying there were no vacancies at London Zoo – but he was offered the job of Relief Keeper at the Society's country zoo at Whipsnade, with the title of his position aptly renamed Student Keeper; Gerry's exceptional background had been recognised and now he was to be given structured training, a sort of university of animals, that would confirm him on the course he had chosen for his life since he was a child.

* * *

At the outbreak of the war, when Leslie was getting on for twenty-three, he attempted to enlist in the Royal Air Force but a damaged eardrum he suffered in a fight as a child at Dulwich College caused the medical board to rule him unfit for military service. Instead he was assigned to a humdrum job working in a local aircraft factory.

There was no adventure for Leslie, except for his secret liaison with Maria Condos, the family maid. He had taken a photograph of her in Corfu and on the reverse he had written 'Jolly nice'.

Now when Margo returned from Africa at the end of the war she noticed Maria putting the washing on the line.

'That's funny, she's pregnant, and I said to Mother, "I think Maria's pregnant," and she looked immediately round for a double gin.'

Epilogue: **Family, Friends and Animals ...**

GERRY BEGAN WRITING *My Family and Other Animals* in 1955 in the attic of his sister's house in Bournmouth at 51 St Alban's Avenue, opposite Mother at number 52. Separated from Jack Breeze, and with two young sons to support, Margo had bought the house in 1947 with her share of the inheritance from her father. After her adventures in marriage and Africa, her Aunt Prue sensibly declared, 'It will be like a sort of anchor for you: at the moment you are like an old boat being tossed about without a rudder.' There was no stability in marriage, continued Prue, not with your temperament, but a guest house would ensure both a home and an income for the rest of your life. Mind you, a guest house, not a boarding house – 'boarding is so common', said Aunt Prue.

Margo felt she was slipping into the shoes of her mother. 'I've always been head of the family – all my life! It has been my burden that I have to carry. And help out here and there wherever needed, wherever there was a drama – and we've had plenty of those.'

One immediate problem would be dealing with Gerry, who, while he was away at Whipsnade Zoo, had 'marked his territorial claim' at Mother's house, 'not with musk and urine but with a marmoset which, happily, did both for him'. Margo had always been tolerant of Gerry and his habits, but 'it was obvious that I should never keep a lodger if I allowed him to put one foot over the threshold of my new house with any species of animal – domestic or otherwise'.

Margo's Bournemouth guest house at 51 St Alban's Avenue: top, Gerry and Jacquie in the garden; below: Margo with her sons, Nicholas and Gerry.

But of course it did not turn out like that. 'In the end we had all the animals, running all over the place.' Over the coming years as Gerald travelled in search of wildlife in Africa and South America, then returned to Bournemouth, where he and his wife Jacquie Wolfenden, whom he married in 1951, inhabited their small room at 51 St Alban's Avenue, a zoo grew up in Margo's back garden – 'monkeys and birds, you name it.'

* * *

Gerry's career as an independent zoologist began when he turned twenty-one and came into his share of the inheritance left by his father; by the end of 1947 he was financing his own wildlife collecting expedition to Cameroon in West Africa. With the animals he brought back he supplied zoos in London, Bristol, Manchester and elsewhere, providing more than twenty-five new species to London Zoo alone. In 1949 Gerry was again in Cameroon and in 1950 he mounted an expedition to Guyana in South America. Unlike other wildlife collecting expeditions, Gerry never over-collected specimens nor aimed to capture animals because they would attract the highest prices from collectors; moreover he fed and housed his animals to the highest standards; which taken all together meant he was broke by the end of the third expedition.

In desperation and encouraged by Jacquie, and with advice from Larry, Gerry turned to writing humorous accounts of his expeditions. *The Overloaded Ark*, published in 1953, was about the first Cameroon expedition and became a bestseller. 'My youngest brother Gerry has scored a tremendous success with his first book and is making a deal of money,' Larry wrote to Henry Miller. 'He collects wild animals for zoos and writes up his adventures afterwards. The one pays for the other; how marvellous to have one's career fixed at 25 or so and to be able to pay one's way.'

Two further bestsellers followed. *Three Singles to Adventure*, about the Guyana expedition, was published in 1954, and *The Bafut Beagles*, about Cameroon again, was published at the end of the same year. Soon Larry was writing to Henry that Gerry was now 'a more famous writer than all of us put together'. But Gerry, who disliked writing, forever looked up to Larry, who at this stage in his career was well regarded within literary circles, but not famous and certainly not able to make a living from his writings. 'The subtle difference between us', Gerry said of Larry, 'is that he loves writing and I don't. To me it's simply a way to do my animal work, nothing more.'

* * *

At the end of the war Larry left Alexandria and was posted to Rhodes as Public Information Officer until the British, who had liberated the island from the Germans, united it with Greece two years later. His sojourn in Rhodes would result in his book about the island, *Reflections on a Marine Venus*, eventually published in 1953. But meanwhile, in 1947, on his way to a new job in Argentina, this time as lecturer at the British Council Institute at Cordoba, Larry came to Bournemouth with his Alexandrian wife Eve and they moved in with Mother at number 52. It was the first time that all the family had been together since Corfu – and it would be the last. Eve responded to the family in the same way Nancy had done fifteen years before, enjoying their banter, their extravagant playfulness and Mother's delicious curries, which she would make at the drop of a hat. 'They all looked alike – all like their mother', Eve thought. The only difference between them was that Gerry was taller than Larry, taller than any of them; Leslie and Larry were about the same size.

In September 1947 Nancy wrote to Mother saying she would like to visit. In August she had married Edward Hodgkin, director of the British-run Near East Arab Broadcasting Station

Eve Cohen Durrell – Larry's second wife and the model for Justine in his *Alexandria Quartet*.

in Jerusalem, and now they had returned to England. Nancy was pregnant and felt that dealing with both seven-year-old Penelope, her daughter by Larry, and her new marriage and an expected child, was too much. So she decided to place Penelope in a school near Bournemouth. Mother averted Nancy's visit with the reply that Larry and Eve were there. But Larry leapt at the chance to see Penelope for the first time since she was two and, recognising that she was feeling abandoned, was soon bringing her home on visits to Mother's at number 52. Penelope was the link that connected Nancy with the family, but there was Margo, too; thirty-six years later, when Nancy was suffering from cancer, Penelope cared for her during that last year and Margo was with her on the day she died.

Leslie had only recently moved out of number 52. With his inheritance he had bought a fishing boat; and with his luck it sank in Poole harbour during its maiden voyage. Now he had moved in with Doris, eleven years older than Leslie, 'big-

Leslie with his wife, Doris, in Bournemouth.

hearted, big-voiced, laughing Doris,' as Gerry called her, who ran the pub down the bottom of the road. Eventually they married – 'when really he should have been marrying Maria, that was my opinion', said Margo, 'but you see, he was already involved with Doris who was a very strong character'.

Maria Condos, whom the family had brought with them from Corfu, gave birth to Leslie's son, Anthony (Tony), in September 1945. 'Leslie didn't really seem to take it too seriously,' recalled Margo, while Maria 'adored him, and used to call him *Roula Mou*, that's Greek for darling, in fact deeper, more tender than darling. It was such an awkward situation; you bring a Greek maid back and, suddenly, find she's expecting, you know, and I arranged for her to go to a home to have the baby. I kept in touch with her and when I had number 51 I had her to stay, and right to her death I was put down as her next of kin.' Tony had memories of monkeys climbing over the furniture and snakes in chests of drawers, but he had no reollection of his father. Maria and Tony eventually moved into a council house in Bournemouth, but it was always a hard life for his mother, who struggled to raise him while working in the laundry at the local Christchurch Hospital.

In 1952 Leslie and Doris went off to Kenya, where he managed a farm, then worked as a bursar at a school, where he misapproprated funds. In order to avoid prosecution, he and Doris fled back to England in 1968, arriving with nothing more than the clothes they wore and £75 in their pockets. Nevertheless, for Margo, Leslie always remained what he had been with her in childhood, 'a lovable rogue'. Leslie did manage to secure a living and a place to live when he got a job as a janitor in a block of flats near Marble Arch in London. He died in 1982 of a heart attack in a pub in Notting Hill Gate, where he would tell everyone that he was a civil engineer.

* * *

Back in Bournemouth, in 1947, Larry met up with Alan Thomas for the first time since before the war; Thomas was now the owner of Commins bookshop, had bought a large house near the centre of town, and was well on his way to becoming the doyen of antiquarian book dealers in Britain. Alan was like an anchor for Larry, also a bank vault and a library; throughout his peripatetic and sometimes perilous career Larry could rely on Alan to safeguard his notebooks and manuscripts and his workimg library, or order books for him. As well as looking after Larry's material, Alan established his own extensive collection of Larry's books and letters, which at his death he bequeathed to the British Library.

From time to time Larry and Eve would go up to London, staying at the home of a friend. It was there that they had his publisher T.S. Eliot to dinner, Eve preparing an excellent Egyptian meal. Larry and Eve also went round to see Veronica Tester, one of the dancers who had visited him on Corfu. Veronica was no longer a ballerina; after the outbreak of war she worked for Tom Harrisson, 'the barefoot anthropologist' and founder of Mass Observation, which gave her an interest in sociology. But then she was called up and given the task of organising the Land Army in the remote countryside of Pembrokeshire. Finally, after the war she enrolled at the London School of Economics, studying sociology and mental health. Larry and Veronica's husband, who was still in the military, 'just sort of glared at each other the way chaps do, and I never saw Larry again'. In any case Veronica felt uncomfortable meeting Larry in the company of Eve: 'To me, Nancy was who belonged with Larry.'

Nancy turned out to have been right about the two dancers; Veronica, she thought, was too large, but Dorothy Stevenson had the right body for a ballerina. After leaving Corfu, Dot, as Veronica always called her friend, joined the Ballets Russes, the most celebrated company of its day, but when war broke out she returned to Australia, where with Edouard Borovansky,

Gerry's mentor Theodore Stephanides with Alan Thomas in London.

a former soloist with the Pavlova company, her brilliance as a dancer and choreographer inspired the development of ballet in her home country. It was said that when she danced a phrase, it stayed danced, holding its shape in the mind's eye.

Also in London, just before he and Eve sailed for Argentina, Larry bumped into Gerry, who was waiting for his cargo ship to take him on his first expedition to Cameroon. Larry was meeting up with Theodore Stephanides; they had seen each other at intervals throughout the war, and now Theodore was settled in London with Mary and Alexia and was working as a radiologist at St Thomas's Hospital, where he would remain until his retirement in 1961. But for Gerry this was the first time he had met his old mentor since leaving Corfu in 1939, 'without whom I would have achieved nothing', as Gerry later said, a friendship now renewed, and to be conjured afresh when he would come to write *My Family and Other Animals*.

Larry's voyage to Argentina turned out to be a disaster. From Cordoba he wrote to a friend, 'Oh dear, this boring tedious town. Food very good. Easy life, but the climate is desperately exacerbatng – electrical storms four times a week – temperatures going up and down ... It is so hard to write about Greece from here' – he was trying to write *Reflections on a Marine Venus*, his book about Rhodes – 'one's feelings don't rise in this climate, the death dew settles on one.' Simply, he was away from the Mediterranean, whose islands and shores had become his home. Cutting short his contract after a year, he and Eve were back in England.

On his return from Argentina, Larry accepted a Foreign Office appointment as press attaché at the British Embassy in Belgrade, where he arrived with Eve in May 1949. At least it was within reach of Greece, where Larry and Eve would drive for their holidays. Two years later, in 1951, Eve gave birth to their daughter Sappho; but towards the end of 1952 Eve was taken to a British military hospital in Germany after falling into a deep depression and suffering hallucinations, which had Larry fearing for their daughter's life.

Larry had hated Argentina and disliked Yugoslavia almost as much; it paled alongside the Mediterranean world he had discovered in Corfu. The work held no great appeal, either. Larry resigned his Foreign Office position and determined to write the book he had sketched out ten years earlier in Alexandria and which would become *Justine*, the first volume of *The Alexandria Quartet*.

He and Eve had been preparing to go to Cyprus, where they could live cheaply on his savings, but in the event Eve continued under medical treatment in England, and early in 1953 Larry travelled alone with Sappho to Cyprus, where Louisa Durrell arrived in May to help look after the child.

That July, Gerry's first book, *The Overloaded Ark*, was published in London, followed a month later by Larry's *Reflections on a Marine Venus*, about Rhodes. However, the cost of rebuilding an old house Larry bought in Bellapais, a mountain village in northern Cyprus, overlooking Kyrenia and the sea, obliged him to earn some money to staunch the drain on his savings. He found a job in the capital, Nicosia, teaching at the Pancyprian Gymnasium, and would rise each morning at 4.30am to write, before driving the thirty miles over twisting mountain roads to begin his job at seven-thirty.

The following April, 1954, Eve felt well enough to come to Cyprus, though tensions between her and Mother led Louisa to return to Bournemouth. At the same time Larry accepted the post of Director of Information Services for the Cyprus government. Part of his responsibilities were the Cyprus Tourist

Eve, Sappho, Larry and Mother at Bellapaix in Cyprus

Office and the Cyprus Broadcasting Station and the monthly magazine *Cyprus Review*, which Larry edited, assisted by his deputy editor George Wilkinson, Gerry's old tutor in Corfu.

During the working week, Larry lived in a small house in Nicosia, returning at weekends to Eve and Sappho at Bellapais.

* * *

While Larry's work on *Justine* was held up by these professional and personal concerns, Gerry's *The Bafut Beagles*, another bestseller, was published in London in October. Then, a few days later, in a letter of 24 October 1954, Gerry wrote to Larry, outlining a grand scheme – he had decided to establish his own zoo and wanted Larry's help.

> I wish to propound an idea to you on which I should like your help and co-operation. I am now, I think, sufficiently well known to attempt something which I have had in mind for a number of years. To you, no doubt, it will sound completely mad and a lot of rubbish. I want to start a Trust or organisation, with land in somewhere like the West Indies, for the breeding of those forms of animal life which are on the borders of extinction, and which without help of this sort cannot survive.

Gerry's fundamental belief, radical at the time, was that zoos should be for the benefit of animals, not for the entertainment of man – they were to be places where animals could be protected, where species could be preserved, numbers grown, and threatened creatures re-established in the wild. Gerry explained to Larry that he had spoken to Julian Huxley, the evolutionary biologist, who thought it an excellent and necessary idea, but Huxley pointed out that, though Gerry could get every well-known zoologist on his side, they did not have money. So, Gerry continued to Larry, 'What I would like to know from you is, who do you know that is stinking rich?'

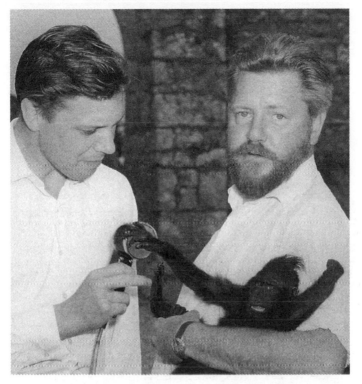

The young media naturalists: Gerry with David Attenborough.

At the end of 1954 Larry invited Gerry to write an article in *The Cyprus Review* about the potential for establishing a zoo on the island. 'It strikes me as surpising that no one has yet started a zoo in a place like Cyprus ... The advantages are considerable, the main one being the climate. It is amazing how a good climate can cut down the costs of such a project, and most creatures, including some of the more rare or delicate beasts, could be bred there with success.'

On 31 March 1955, Gerry arrived in Cyprus to see for himself. Larry arranged a cocktail party that evening to introduce Gerry to Cypriot society. Then, just after midnight, as the brothers were having a drink, the thunder of blasting bombs rolled through the streets of Nicosia, and like seismic aftershocks reports came in of more explosions in Limassol, Larnaca and Famagusta. Archbishop Makarios, leader of the Greek Cypriot community, had given the order to General Grivas, leader of EOKA, the National Organisation of Cypriot Fighters, to begin the terrorist campaign whose aim was the union or *enosis* of Cyprus with Greece. Over the next two years hundreds of people, mostly Cypriots, would die at the hands of EOKA; Larry himself was nearly killed by a terrorist's bullet and an incendiary bomb was placed in his garage.

In July, Eve left Larry and, taking Sappho with her, went to England. In that same summer another Alexandrian, Claude Vincendon, joined the French section of the Cyprus Broadcasting Corporation. She was a writer 'with something oddly her own', Larry wrote to Henry Miller. 'She tumbled into my arms and gave me enough spark to settle down and demolish the book.'

> I used to make her come round to the villa at bomb time and set up a typewriter on the dining table. We drank red wine and worked like maniacs. Every twenty minutes there was a boom and something in the town went up; the telephone rang. We disregarded everything. I answered the duty room, the staff room, Government House, Police Press – and back to *Justine*.

Night after night they sat working on their books, their typewriters at opposite ends of the table, on which they spread a map of Alexandria, 'tracing and re-tracing the streets with our fingers, recapturing much that I had lost, the brothels and the parks, the dawns over Lake Mareotis'. Against the noise of pistol shots and bombs going off at the rate of three or four a night, and of reports coming in from the operations room of another ambush in the mountains, it was a 'very queer and thrilling period, sad, weighed down with futility and disgust, but marvellous to be able to live in one's book'.

Claude, whom Larry met in Cyprus after his marriage to Eve collapsed.

Justine was finished, but so was Cyprus for Larry, and that summer he returned to England. Then, in early 1957, having lost all hope of making Cyprus his new Greek island home, he and Claude went to live in Sommieres, in Provence, where Larry remained for the rest of his life. *Justine* would be the making of his reputation as a novelist – the first volume of *The Alexandria Quartet*, which would be acclaimed around the world.

* * *

At the same time as Larry was writing *Justine*, Gerry was writing his own masterpiece in his small attic room at Margo's house in Bournemouth, recovering the Corfu he thought he had lost with childhood. As with his other books, Gerry set out to write a straightforward money-earning animal book, first calling it *Childhood with Scorpions*, then *World in a Nautilus*, and running through several more titles as the writing progressed. But increasingly the family imposed itself on the book until finally he arrived at the title, *My Family and Other Animals*.

'The book was written sitting in bed in my sister's house, with an endless procession of family and friends coming into the room to gossip, drink tea or wine, fight or just simply tell me how the book should be written,' Gerry recalled. He claimed to be astonished that he had managed to write anything at all, yet he found this book – unlike its predecessors – a joy to write, even suggesting that it was effortlessly written by some secret spirit within him.

When he had completed it, the first thing Gerry did was send a copy of the typescript to Theodore to check it for the biology and history of Corfu and the correct spelling of Greek names. Meanwhile the family was reading the book with differing reactions. Mother hardly recognised herself and complained, 'The awful thing about Gerald's book is that I'm beginning to believe it is all true.' Larry, for his part, praised Gerry's essential truthfulness: 'He has successfully recreated his family with the devastatingly faithful eye of a thirteen year old. This is a very wicked, very funny, and I'm afraid rather truthful book.'

For Margo, who felt Gerry portrayed her as a walking non sequitur and something of an airhead, forever worried about pimple cream: 'There were things I objected to strongly'; what she called exaggerations. 'Gerry took it for absolute granted that I would sanction everything he wrote, but I didn't. Gerry became very successful by libelling me a lot.'

By the time *My Family and Other Animals* was published, Leslie had long gone to Kenya and left no recorded reaction to the book. But Gerry, talking some years later to his friend David Hughes, said it was Leslie who had taught him what storytelling was all about. It had started when Leslie would

The Family – Leslie aside – reunited: Gerry, Margo, Mother and Larry, at Gerry's zoo on Jersey, Christmas 1960.

return home from school on holidays 'and tell me Billy Bunter stories. He used to embellish them with his own bits and pieces, add a dash of his own school adventures, imitate a master or two in a very clever and vivid fashion. He had the same gift as Larry, only untutored, not so well developed.'

And more than that. Gerry paid Leslie the compliment of stealing at least one of his stories for inclusion in *My Family and Other Animals*. It was not, in fact, Gerry who encountered and was befriended by Kosti the convict and murderer. That story was Leslie's; Gerry simply appropriated Leslie's story to himself. Which was something of a family habit. Larry liked to tell the story of being treated for tropical sprue in India and having to drink the warm blood from a freshly killed chicken, but again the event belonged to Leslie; he had been the sickly child who was made to drink the chicken's blood.

* * *

Defeated by violence from founding his zoo in Cyprus, Gerry hoped to start a zoo in Bournemouth or Poole, but in 1958 after months of negotiations he was thwarted again, this time by what he called the 'constipated mentality of local government'. Gerry was about to abandon the idea of a zoo altogether when his publisher told him that he had a contact in Jersey who might be able to help him find someplace there. Gerry flew to the island and was met at the airport by Major Hugh Fraser, who took him back for lunch at his ancestral home, Les Augrès Manor, in Trinity. There, Gerry almost idly said this would make a fine place for a zoo, to which the Major replied, 'Are you serious?' and suddenly the deal was done. 'So after a frustrating year of struggling with councils and other local authorities, I had gone to Jersey and within an hour of landing at the airport I had found my zoo.'

The Jersey zoo would be Mother's home for the last years of her life. At times Louisa's children had seemed like animals, so, as she said, this was nothing new. On one occasion Chumley the chimpanzee escaped from his cage and with his girlfriend Lulu loped across the grounds to the manor house and up the stairs. Mother heard a loud bang on her door and found them cheerfully standing there, looking for a cuddle and treats. She sat them down on the sofa and opened a tin of biscuits and

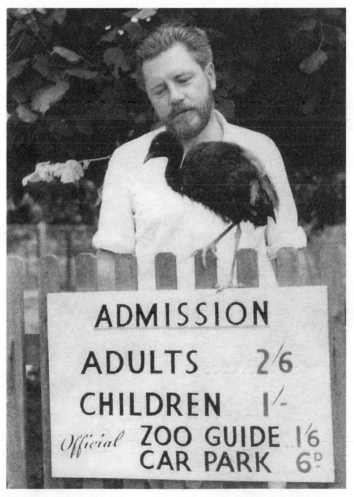

ADMISSION

ADULTS ... 2/6
CHILDREN 1/-
Official ZOO GUIDE 1/6
CAR PARK 6ᴰ

Gerry with Trumpy, the Greywinged Trumpeter, opening the Jersey zoo.

a box of chocolates. When Gerry found out he remonstrated with her for letting them in. 'But dear, they came to *tea* – and they had jolly sight better manners than some of the *people* you've had up here.'

On a visit to Bournemouth in 1964, Mother suddenly died.

* * *

The creation of the zoo was miraculous but its survival required hard work. Gerry was obliged to write two books a year to keep it afloat. But he was not the man to manage the finances and administration of such a large and complex project. 'Uncle Gerry had a heart of gold,' said Margo's son Gerry Breeze, who worked at the zoo in its early days, 'but his wife Jacquie was the captain. Handing out orders was not his way of doing things. He was only concerned with the animals, not with administering anything.' Jacquie, however, felt herself on the margins and claimed that Gerry was entirely absorbed in the animals and hardly took account of her. In 1976, she left Gerry and the zoo.

A year later, while visiting Duke University in North Carolina, Gerry met Lee McGeorge, a Zoology graduate who had recently returned from Madagascar, where she had been studying the social behaviour of lemurs and the vocal communication of birds and mammals. Gerry explained how this first encounter went: 'Animal communication in all its forms happened to be a subject in which I was deeply interested. I gazed at her. That she was undeniably attractive was one thing, but to be attractive *and* studying animal communication lifted her almost into the realm of being a goddess.' In 1979 they married, and for the next sixteen years, until his death in 1995, Lee joined Gerry on expeditions, in writing books and in running the zoo. Today, Lee continues to play an active role as honorary director of the Durrell Wildlife Conservation Trust at what had been Jersey Zoo and is now renamed The Durrell Zoo.

Gerry with Lee McGeorge, 1977.

The earliest home to Gerry's zoo in England was at 51 St Alban's Avenue in Bournemouth, the place where he wrote *My Family and Other Animals*. Margo died there in 2004 and the house was sold. No monkeys have been seen in the neighbourhood for years. There ought at least to be a plaque outside.

Following the publication of *The Alexandria Quartet*, Larry was shortlisted for the 1962 Nobel Prize for Literature. He

The acclaimed novelist: Lawrence Durrell in Paris, 1984.

revisited the Greece of his youth in the 1976 BBC film *Spirit of Place – Lawrence Durrell's Greece*, in which he journeys to Corfu, Rhodes, Crete and Hydra. Meanwhile he had written two dystopian novels, *Tunc* and *Nunquam*, before turning his attention to Provence, where he lived. *Monsieur*, *Livia*, *Constance*, *Sebastian* and *Quinx* comprise his last major work, *The Avignon Quintet*, filled with lyrical and mystical evocations of Provence, with *Constance* in particular being one of the best novels about France during the Second World War. In 1990 Larry, who had been living for some years with his last partner, Francoise Kestsman, died in Sommieres.

* * *

The Durrell Zoo in Jersey and Gerry's *My Family and Other Animals* are the legacy of a magical childhood in Corfu. And Larry's *Prospero's Cell*, which lyrically captures the atmosphere of Corfu before the war, ranks with *The Alexandria Quartet* and *Bitter Lemons*, his account of his years in Cyprus, as one of the best books he ever wrote.

Corfu, meantime, has changed. It had already been ruined by tourism, in Gerry's view, by the time he returned in 1967 to make *Corfu, Garden of the Gods*, a BBC television documentary. He felt guilty that perhaps the tourists were following in the footsteps of *My Family and Other Animals*. 'Total lack of control, total rapacity, total insensitivity' was his condemnation of the Greeks who sacrificed beauty to money – the money not even going into local pockets but to tour operators and hotel consortiums. Not only animals can be endangered and wiped out, he lamented, but landscapes too.

The three villas are, in fact, still there – the Strawberry-Pink, the Daffodil-Yellow, the Snow-White – but they are privately owned, cannot be visited (though the first can be rented) and can be hard to find. The airport runway extends to the tip of Canoni, where Spiro Americanos used to live, and planes approach low over Perama and the Chessboard Fields.

But at Kalami there is the White House where Larry and Nancy made their home. As Larry described it:

> That house with its remoteness and the islands going down like soft gongs all the time into the amazing blue, and I shall really never, never ever forget a youth spent there discovered by accident. It was pure gold. But then of course there may be an element of self-deception in it because youth does mean happiness, it does mean love, and that's something you can't get over.

To the side of the White House is a taverna with beautiful views across the bay and towards Albania. The taverna is built upon that black ledge of rock where Nancy and Larry would breakfast early in the morning; where Henry Miller stripped himself naked and swam in the sea for the first time in twenty years; where Theodore observed stars and comets in the night sky; where Veronica and Dorothy danced; where Spiro would descend the goat path from his Dodge on the road above; where Margo sunned and Gerry searched the shallow waters for strange creatures when they came to visit; where Leslie put in with his boat when he took the whole family for a day of hunting, fishing, collecting and picnicking, at Lake Antiniotissa in the far north of the island, so beautiful that Mother gave it her highest accolade: 'I'd like to be buried there.'

The house is owned now by Tassos Athenaios, grandson of Totsa, and his wife Daria – still in family hands. Here you can have a drink and know that everybody has passed by once upon a time.

* * *

Larry sent this photo to Henry Miller in 1947, writing:
"Do you remember Spiro? Here is a picture of him cooking an eel in red sauce for Gerald, then aged about 12. The old car in the background. Just after this was taken the car was nearly carried away by the sea and we had to stand up to our waists in water and dig it out."

Further Reading

Works by the Durrells and Friends

GERALD DURRELL:

Titles with an immediate relevance to Corfu.

My Family and Other Animals, 1956; *Birds, Beasts and Relatives*, 1969; *The Garden of the Gods*, 1978. (Published in one volume as *The Corfu Trilogy*, 2006).

Fillets of Plaice, 1971.

Marrying Off Mother and Other Stories, 1991.

LAWRENCE DURRELL:

Major works or otherwise relevant to Greece.

The Black Book, 1938 – written on Corfu.

Prospero's Cell, 1945 – about Corfu.

Reflections on a Marine Venus, 1953 – about Rhodes.

Bitter Lemons, 1957 – about Cyprus.

The Alexandria Quartet (*Justine*, 1957; *Balthazar*, 1958; *Mountolive*, 1958; *Clea*, 1960).

Spirit of Place, 1969 – Mediterranean travel writing.

Blue Thirst, 1975 – about Corfu and Egypt.

The Greek Islands, 1978.

The Durrell-Miller Letters 1935-80, 1988.

Lawrence Durrell Selected Poems edited by Peter Porter, 2006.

MARGARET DURRELL

Whatever Happened to Margo?, 1995.

HENRY MILLER
The Colossus of Maroussi, 1941.

THEODORE STEPHANIDES
Autumn Gleanings: Corfu Memoirs and Poems, 2011.

Works about the Durrells

Douglas Botting *Gerald Durrell: The Authorised Biography*, 1999.

David Hughes *Himself and Other Animals: A Portrait of Gerald Durrell*, 1997.

Ian MacNiven *Lawrence Durrell: A Biography*, 1998.

Joanna Hodgkin *Amateurs in Eden: The Story of a Bohemian Marriage: Nancy and Lawrence Durrell*, 2012.

Michael Haag *Alexandria: City of Memory*, 2004.

ONLINE

Durrell Wildlife Conservation Trust
www.durrell.org

The Ark Gallery
www.arkgallery.org

Durrelliana: a Scrapbook
www.whitemetropolis.wordpress.com

The International Lawrence Durrell Society
www.lawrencedurrell.org

Acknowledgments

My special thanks to Lee Durrell and the Durrell Wildlife Conservation Trust for generously allowing me access to Gerald Durrell's family photographs and his papers, in particular his notes for his unpublished autobiography. Family and other interviews with Margaret Durrell and also memoirs written by her were kindly made available to me by her granddaughter Tracy Breeze and her niece Penelope Durrell Hope

Thanks also to the following people who in various ways have kindly contributed towards the writing of this book, in some cases before I knew I was going to write it:

Tassos and Daria Athenaios, Gerry Breeze, Tracy Breeze, Catherine Brown, Brewster Chamberlin, Veronica Tester Dane, Eve Cohen Durrell, Jacquie Durrell, Lawrence Durrell, Anthony Hirst, Joanna Hodgkin, Penelope Durrell Hope, Françoise Kestsman, Ian MacNiven, Alexia Mercouri, Alexander Mercouris, Anthea Morton-Saner, Simon Nye, Frank Pike, Richard Pine, Dorothy Stevenson Rumsey, Charles Sligh, Alan Thomas, Rev Alistair Tresider at St Luke's Church, Hampstead, Nanos Valaoritis, and Rev Jules Wilson at Holy Trinity Church, Corfu.

I would like to thank for their assistance: the British Library, the Gennadius Library in Athens, the Morris Library at Southern Illinois University at Carbondale, the University of Victoria Library in British Columbia, the University of California Los Angeles Library, and l'Université Paris X at Nanterre.

Sources and images

The following works have been quoted in this book

GERALD DURRELL

My Family and Other Animals, 1956; *Birds, Beasts and Relatives*, 1969; *The Garden of the Gods*, 1978. All copyright Gerald Durrell:

LAWRENCE DURRELL

Pied Piper of Lovers, 1935; *The Black Book*, 1938; *Prospero's Cell*, 1945; *Spirit of Place*, 1969; *Blue Thirst*, 1975; *The Durrell-Miller Letters 1935-80*, 1988. All copyright Lawrence Durrell excepting letters by Henry Miller.

OTHERS

Autumn Gleanings: Corfu Memoirs and Poems by Theodore Stephanides, 2011 (copyright Theodore Stephanides).

The Colossus of Maroussi by Henry Miller, 1941 (copyright Henry Miller).

Golden Threads by Benjamin Rossen. *Recollections of the Durrells* by Vivian Iris Raymond (www.levantineheritage.com)(copyright Benjamin Rossen)

PHOTOGRAPHS AND ILLUSTRATIONS

Index

Durrell Wildlife Conservation Trust

'Gerry Durrell was, to use the modern idiom, Magic,' said his friend and fellow naturalist Sir David Attenborough. 'You imbibe it in his books, you feel it in his Zoo, you see it in the eyes of his trainees, and you hear it in even the most restrained tones of zoo directors.'

Gerry founded the Durrell Wildlife Park (originally called Jersey Zoo) in 1959 and created the Durrell Wildlife Conservation Trust in 1963 with the mission of saving species from extinction. (Its name was changed from the Jersey Wildlife Preservation Trust after his death). The Trust continues his work today, running the Zoo in Jersey to pioneer conservation work, as well as Field Programmes around the world and a Conservation Academy.

Visit the Trust's website (www.durrell.org) for more on the species that the Durrell Trust has helped preserve – or, better still, visit the Wildlife Park in Jersey which also has an exhibit on Gerry's life (including the original manuscript of *My Family and Other Animals*). The Trust welcomes support and animal adoptions.

durrell